The Robert Collier Copywriting Course

In Ten Lessons

Second Edition

Written, Edited, Updated and Revised by Dr. Robert C. Worstell,

including material by Robert Collier

AF434864

While every precaution has been taken in the preparation of this book, the publisher assumes no responsibility for errors or omissions, or for damages resulting from the use of the information contained herein.

THE ROBERT COLLIER COPYWRITING COURSE

First edition. May 25, 2020.

Copyright © 2020, 2022 Dr. Robert C. Worstell.

Written, Edited, and Compiled by Dr. Robert C. Worstell. Includes material by Robert Collier from his Letter Book

Table of Contents

To all our many devoted and loyal fans:

We find and publish these stories <u>only</u> for you.

(Be sure to get your bonuses at the end of the story...)

Forward

ALMOST A HUNDRED YEARS ago, Robert Collier made his living sending out sales letters by post directly to individuals. And it was a very good living. His record was such that even today, people want to learn how he did that.

The trick was in his basics. The rules are as old as time, yet many people won't take the time to distill their own and their competition's craft to discover what works routinely.

Those who do, are way ahead of the rest of the field.

Collier, among several others listed in the Bibliography, took some time to write a book on his successes. This "Letter Book", as he called it, has been in and out of print ever since. While it was a massive book all on it's own, we've taken the time to distill the 10 main lessons that Collier taught in that book and re-published them here.

What we are doing with all the books in this Masters of Marketing series is to apply the modern publication technology of ebooks and Print on Demand to ensure that these book never go unavailable again.

As we've been working at these, we've also found that each of them can be distilled to a few simple lessons. Courses are being created, in order of the most popular books, so students of copywriting and advertising can more readily absorb and internalize the success principles these classic authors have proved for themselves.

As you cross-compare these books, you'll see that Collier was well ahead of later successes like Eugene Schwartz in direct order methods through the mail. But the principles they used were almost exactly the same.

Again, this short series of books is from the most successful copywriters and marketers of their period. The ones who wrote books about what they found successful. Usually, it was a single volume. That just gives us more reason to keep these books in circulation.

And so, let's let you get on with your expanding education, as you stand on the shoulders of another giant to see further.

Dr. Robert C. Worstell, Editor

Preface

THIS IS NOT A TEXTBOOK, calculated to show the beginner how to take his pen or typewriter in hand and indite a masterly epistle to some fancied customer.

It is for the business man who already knows the theory of letter writing but is looking for more effective ways of putting it into practice.

It covers all the necessary rules, of course, but it does this informally.

Primarily, it is the log book of a long and varied experience.

It shows successful ways of selling all manner of products. But through all the differences in products and appeals, runs this one connecting thread—that while products and reasons for buying may vary, human nature remains much the same; that familiarity with the thing you are selling is an advantage, but the one essential without which success is impossible in selling, by mail or selling in person, is a thorough understanding of human reactions.

Study your reader first—your product second. If you understand his reactions, and present those phases of your product that relate to his needs, then you cannot help but write a good letter.

It may be said of this book that it does not give enough examples of unsuccessful letters. But most of us can find plenty of these in our own files.

And isn't it true that we are far less concerned with why a letter failed than in finding out what it is that makes a letter successful?

Robert Collier

New York, N. Y. May, 1931.

Chapter 1 -
WHAT IS IT THAT MAKES SOME LETTERS PAY?

WHAT IS THERE ABOUT some letters that makes them so much more effective than others?

A letter may have perfect diction, a finished style; it may bristle with attention-getters and interest-arousers; it may follow every known rule; yet when it reaches the Hall of Judgment where the reader sits and decides its fate, it may find itself cast into the hell of wastebasket-dom, while some screed lacking any pretense of polish or the finer arts of correspondence, blandly picks up the bacon and walks home with it. Why?

Because getting the results you set out to accomplish with a letter is no more a matter of rule of thumb than is landing a fish with a rod and hook. You know how often you have seen some ragged urchin pull in fish after fish with the crudest of lines, when a "sportsman" near by, though armed with every piscatorial lure known to man, could not raise even a bite!

It's a matter of bait, that's all. The youngster knew what the fish would bite on, and he gave it to them. Result? A mess of fine fish for dinner. The "sportsman" offered them what he had been led to believe fish ought to have—and they turned up their fishy noses at it.

Hundreds of books have doubtless been written about the fine art of fishing, but the whole idea is contained in that one sentence: "What bait will they bite on?" Thousands of articles have been written about the way to use letters to bring you what you want, but the meat of them all can be compressed into two sentences: "What is the bait that will tempt your reader? How can you tie up the thing you have to offer with that bait?"

For the ultimate purpose of every business letter simmers down to this:

The reader of this letter wants certain things. The desire for them is, consciously or unconsciously, the dominant idea in his mind all the time.

You want him to do a certain definite thing for you. How can you tie this up to the thing he wants, in such a way that the doing of it will bring him a step nearer to his goal?

It matters not whether you are trying to sell him a rain-coat, making him a proposal of marriage, or asking him to pay a bill. In each case, you want him to do something for you. Why should he? Only because of the hope that the doing of it will bring him nearer his heart's desire, or the fear that his failure to do it will remove that heart's desire farther from him.

Put yourself in his place. If you were deep in discussion with a friend over some matter that meant a great deal to both of you, and a stranger came up, slapped you on the back and said: "See here, Mister, I have a fine coat I want to sell you!" What would you do? Examine the coat with interest, and thank him for the privilege, or kick him and the coat down the nearest stairs, and blister both with a few choice adjectives in the process?

Well, much the same thing happens when you approach a man by mail. He is deep in a discussion with himself over ways and means of getting certain things that mean a great deal to him. You butt in (that is the only term that describes it) and blandly tell him to forget those things that so deeply concern him and consider your proposition instead. Is it any wonder he promptly tells you where to head in, and lacking the ability to reach you, takes it out on your letter instead?

Then what is the right way to approach him? How would you do it if you were approaching him in person? If he were talking to someone, you'd listen for a while, wouldn't you, and get the trend of the conversation? Then when you chimed in, it would be with a remark on some related subject, and from that you would bring the talk around logically to the point you wanted to discuss. It should not be much more difficult in a letter. There are certain prime human emotions with which the thoughts of all of us are occupied a goodly part of the time. Tune in on them, and you have your reader's attention. Tie it up to the thing you have to offer, and you are sure of his interest.

You see, your reader glancing over his mail is much like a man in a speeding train. Something catches his eye and he turns for a better look. You have his attention. But attention alone gets you nowhere. The something must stand closer inspection, it must win his interest, otherwise his attention is lost— and once lost, it is twice as hard to win the second time. Again it's a matter of bait—you may attract a fish's attention with a gaudily painted bauble, but if he once nibbles it and finds it made of tin, you will have a hard time reaching him again with anything else of the same kind.

Every mail brings your reader letters urging him to buy this or that, to pay a bill, to get behind some movement or to try a new device. Time was when the mere fact that an envelope looked like a personal letter addressed to him would have intrigued his interest. But that time has long since passed.

Letters as letters are no longer objects of intense interest. They are bait neither more nor less—and to tempt him, they must look a bit different from bait he has nibbled at and been fooled by before. They must have something about them that stands out from the mass—that catches his eye and arouses his interest—or away they go into the wastebasket.

Your problem, then, is to find a point of contact with his interests, his desires, some feature that will flag his attention and make your letter stand out from all others the moment he reads the first line.

But it won't do to yell "Fire!" That will get you attention, yes of a kind but as far as your prospects of doing business are concerned, it will be of the kind a drunken miner got in the days when the West wore guns and used them on the slightest provocation. He stuck his head in the window of a crowded saloon and yelled "Fire!"— *and everybody did!*

Study your reader. Find out what interests him. Then study your proposition to see how it can be made to tie in with that interest. Take as an instance, the mother of a month-old baby. What is most in her thoughts? Imagine, then, how a letter starting like this would appeal to her:

After baby's food and baby's clothes, the most important thing you have to decide upon is the little cart baby is going to ride in—is going to be seen in is going to be admired in.

Never a child came into the world but was worthy as good a cart, etc.

Or if you were the father of a six or eight-year-old boy, wouldn't this get under your skin?

Your boy is a little shaver now. He thinks you are the most wonderful man in the world. You can fix his boat, mend his velocipede, tell him wonderful stories.

But it will be only ten or twelve years until he goes to College. The fathers of the other boys—his chums—will go to see them. There will be a Railroad President, perhaps; a great Banker; a Governor.

And you will go; and your boy will say, "This is my *father, boys.*" How will he feel when he says it? Will he be proud of you?

Or take any one of the following starts. Can't you just see your reader nodding in interested agreement, can't you picture the way they would carry him along into a description of the thing offered, how they would make him want it, how they would lead him on to the final action?

To a Druggist

After you have run up front half a dozen times to sell a couple of stogies, a package of court plaster and a postage stamp; to change a five dollar bill for the barber, to answer the phone and inform Mrs. Smith that Castoria is 250 a bottle, and assure Mrs. Jones that you will have the doctor call her up as soon as he comes in, then take a minute for yourself and look over this proposition. It's worthwhile.

To a Householder

Doesn't it beat the Dutch the way thieves, pick-pockets, hold-up men and burglars are getting away with it these days?

There were over 1500 house burglaries last month in our dear old city; 92 business burglaries; 122 street hold-ups; 11 offices held up; 309 automobiles stolen, and the Lord only knows how many watches and purses taken on the streets. A good insurance policy against burglary and theft is a pretty cheap investment these days. Call me on the phone now, and I can have your valuables covered by noon.

To a Farmer

Any man who owns a cow loses a calf once in a while. If you own a herd of a dozen or more, you are probably losing one or two calves a year. We know of breeders who were losing every calf—some sixteen—some over thirty a year.

And these breeders stopped their losses short—just like that—through the information given by us.

To a Merchant

"She didn't buy anything."

How often is this little tragedy repeated in your store?

Your time is valuable your overhead expense runs on—and it costs you real money when a prospective customer walks out of your store without making a purchase.

To a Mother

About that boy of yours— He is arriving at the age when his spirit of manliness asserts itself. You find him imitating his father's manners—he is using your embroidery scissors to shave with—he is no longer ambitious to be a policeman, but has his eye on the Presidency. Among the serious problems with him today is this: He is beginning to want manly, square-cut, "growing-up" clothes. He is no longer satisfied with ordinary boys' clothes, He wants something "like father's."

To a Motorist

If you have ever driven your car in a rainstorm, you know how annoying it is—dangerous, too—to have your wind shield clouded with water. How many times have you narrowly avoided accidents under these conditions?

With the — Cleaner attached to your car, all you need to do is turn a button in front of you, and instantly every drop of water in your field of vision is swept from your wind shield. The glass is left clear and clean.

To a Doctor

What a clutter of books a doctor can get around him, and what a fearful outlay of money they will come to represent if he doesn't use great discrimination in their purchase. I don't suppose there is any class of people—and I have customers among every class you can think of—who appreciate more than my medical friends the marvelous savings I am able to make them on all standard sets, reference books, etc.

To a Housewife

After you have your breakfast dishes washed, your floors swept, and your beds made up, I should like to have a moment of your time. You are an excellent judge of what is good to eat, and know when you are getting what you should from your grocer to be saving and yet to set your table with healthful and dainty dishes for your family...

To Any Man

Are you like Mr. Fuller in that you dislike to shave with cold or lukewarm water?

Mr. Fuller always grumbled when the water was cold. Usually it was cold.

You know how the ordinary hot water system works early in the morning.

But the Fullers found a way out of their troubles. Now—nowadays, no matter how early they may arise, there's always steaming hot water the instant a faucet is turned.

To Insurance Agents

Did you ever, as a kid, sneak up alongside an old mill pond and heave what Penrod might call a "good old rock" far out into the middle of its placid surface—just for the fun of seeing all the mud turtles on all their sunny legs drop off into the water with one loud, individual PLUNK?

If the humble mud turtle formed no part of the backyard fauna of your youth, I reckon there was something mighty similar to engage your budding talents.

Just as you find now, in your grown-up days, that the pursuit of your business aims often involve the same emotions that lent interest to your activities in the eyes of your early neighbors. For example: We want to point out to you a few of the prospects that are basking along the banks of the . . .

Bait—all of them. Find the thing your prospect is interested in and make it your point of contact, rather than rush in and try to tell him something about your proposition, *your* goods, *your* interests.

Chapter 2 -
HOW TO AROUSE THAT ACQUISITIVE FEELING

TO GO BACK TO THE VERY beginning, what is the first thing to do in writing any business letter?

Before you put pen to paper, before you ring for your stenographer, decide in your own mind what effect you want to produce on your reader—what feeling you must arouse in him.

If you want your readers to say, as the crowds did of Demosthenes' famous rival: "What a clever speaker!"—then it is quite all right to start with catch-phrases and the like. But if you want to emulate Demosthenes, whose hearers forgot all about him in their interest in his message, then your whole effort must be centered on arousing the feeling in them: *"Let's go!"*

For back of every successful letter, as back of every sale, is a created feeling that impels the reader to act as you want him. It is the whole purpose of every business letter, whether it be sales, collection, adjustment or complaint, to make your reader *want* to do the thing you are urging upon him.

How are you to arouse that feeling in him? How would you have to feel yourself before you would place such an order as you have in mind, before you would grant such an extension, before you would send a payment to this man in preference to all others, at a time when it was an effort to send a dollar to anyone?

What would you want first to know? What about the proposition would interest you most? What would you feel you had to gain by accepting? What would you lose by refusing?

They say the Parisians have a formula for love letters: "Begin without knowing what you are going to say, and end without knowing what you have said." That may be good medicine for love letters, but it was never meant for business. Though, to do the Frenchmen justice, such of their letters as appear in print indicate that while they may not know what they are going to say, they have a pretty clear idea of the emotion they want to arouse in their reader, and they leave no stone unturned in the doing of it.

And after all, isn't that the whole purpose of a letter? Books have been written about the importance of attention, and interest, and argument, and clinchers, but aren't these mere details? When you come down to it, isn't the prime requisite arousing the *feeling* in your reader that *he must have* the thing you are offering, or that he can not rest until he has done the thing you are urging him to?

Consider the two following letters, for instance. The first follows all the rules. It wins attention, it creates interest, it describes what it has to offer, it has argument, conviction, clincher, yet it was only moderately successful, whereas the second letter literally pulled its head off. Why the difference?

Because the first letter was aimed only at the intellect, whereas the second, while it tried to convince the intellect, aimed its real appeal at the emotions! And when it is action you want, go after the emotions every time!

The Finally Revised,

Illustrated Edition of WELLS' HISTORY in 4 vols.

At 1/4 less than the Original Price of Two!

DEAR READER:

At last H. G. Wells' famous "Outline of History" has been put into its finally revised form, illustrated with 100 famous historical paintings, and brought out in four regular, library-size books.

A million copies of the Outline were sold in the bulky one and two volume editions. A million more people wanted it, but they waited for a lighter, more easily handled volume. Here it is—a brand new edition, freshly revised, of four standard library-size books, for 25% *less than the price of the original two-volume set.*

And that isn't all.

For a long time Mr. Wells felt that parts of his history needed re-writing— that other parts should be clarified, and the whole thoroughly revised. This was his chance. Starting from the very beginning, he changed every single page of the text, re-wrote whole chapters, added page after page of additional matter. This is his final revision. In discussing this edition with a friend while in America, Mr. Wells said that the revisions would make the original English edition look like a Stone Age effort.

There are a hundred new illustrations, reproductions from historical paintings from the great art galleries of the world. Not only New York, but

the Art Stores and Galleries of London and Paris were searched through for these. It is the finest edition of the "Outline of History" that has ever been brought out. Yet you may have it—if you mail the enclosed card at once—at an amazingly low price.

One-Fourth Off!

Think of it! Finally revised, printed from brand new, clear, readable plates, with a hundred new pictures besides those that were in the discarded editions, and bound up into 4 beautiful, library-size volumes—all for *25%* less than the original two-volume set would cost you even now in any book store!

Here is our offer:

H.G. Wells' remarkable History, the most engrossing story ever told, being the complete romance of Mother Earth, bound up into 4 regular library-size books, illustrated with a hundred famous paintings, and A year's subscription to *the Review of Reviews,*

Both Together for $12

payable in easy, never missed payments of $1 a month, or $10.50 cash.

Wells begins with the dawn of time. Before there were men. Before there were even reptiles. In broad, magnificent strokes he paints the picture, bringing you straight down to today. In a few vivid pages, he brings the whole past back to life, and makes you live through it. More—he makes it all one connected story, shows you the thread of human purpose binding men together the world over from one age to another.

And the Review of Reviews makes the history of today as alive and interesting as Wells makes the years behind us. Without waste of time, it gives you the boiled-down sap of world events, equips you to discuss national and international affairs intelligently, enables you to read your daily paper with real interest and understandingly.

Only One Condition We Make.

There is only one condition—that you send in your card within ten days after you receive this letter. Such an unusual offer as this cannot be held open long. We can give you but the one chance.

Mail the enclosed card, without money, and we will send you, subject to a week's free examination, the new 4-volume Wells' "Outline of History" at 25% less than the original 2-volume price. At the same time, we will enter your subscription for one full year of *the Review of Reviews*. Remember, you don't risk one penny. If for any reason you are dissatisfied with the History, if you don't feel that it gives you the utmost of book value and satisfaction, return it at the end of the week at our expense, send 25 cents for the copy of the magazine delivered to you, and cancel the order.

The enclosed card obligates us only— *Not You!* Signing and mailing it puts the burden of Proof up to us.

May we hope you will *mail it today?*

Earnestly yours,

YOUR LAST CHANCE

to Get These 4 Volumes For 25% LESS

Than the Price of the First Two!

DEAR READER:

Do you know what is the really significant thing about all these pre-historic fossils and ancient civilizations that have been dug up in the past few years?

—Not the fact that the Dinosaur eggs found in Mongolia may be 10,000,000 or 100,000,000 years old.

—Nor whether the Temple of the Moon-God in Ur of the Chaldees was built before the Tower of Babel, or the Temple of the Sun-God in Mexico was more ancient still.

—Not even whether mankind dates back to the primitive Ape-man of 500,000 years ago, or sprang full-grown from the mind of the Creator.

Not these things. They are, after all, of little consequence to us now. The really significant thing is that from them men are, for the first time, beginning to get an understanding of that infinite "life-principle" that moves the universe—and of the untold possibilities it opens up to them.

You read in Wells' "Outline of History" how for millions of years this "life-principle" was threatened by every kind of danger—sudden climactic changes, lack of food, floods, earthquakes, droughts, volcanic eruptions.

But to it each new danger was merely an incentive to finding a new resource.

Pursued through water, it sought land. Pursued over land, it sought the air.

To breath in the sea, it put forth gills. Stranded on land, it made lungs. To protect itself from glacial cold, it grew fur. In temperate climes, hair. Subject to alternate heat and cold, it produced feathers. To meet one danger it developed a shell. For another, fleetness of foot or wing. But ever, from the beginning, it showed its power to meet every creature need.

All through the history of life and mankind you see this same directing Intelligence—call it Nature, call it Providence, call it what you will—rising to meet every need of life.

No man can read Wells' without realizing that the whole purpose of existence is growth—that life is dynamic, not static. That it is ever moving forward—not standing still. That electricity, magnetism, gravitation, light, are all but different manifestations of the same infinite and eternal energy in which we ourselves live and move and have our being.

Wells' gives you an understanding of your own potentialities. You learn from it how to work with and take advantage of the infinite energy all about you. The terror of the man at the crossways, not knowing which road to take, is no terror to the reader of Wells. His future is of his own making. For the only law of infinite energy is the law of supply. The "life-principle" that formed the dinosaur to meet one set of needs and the butterfly to meet another is not going to fail in your case. You have but to understand it—to work in harmony with it—to get from it what you need.

Your Last Chance To Get Wells' At The Low Price

The low price we have been making on Wells' "Outline of History" was made possible only because we contracted for 100,000 sets at once.

Because we were willing to take the risk of paying the royalty on that vast quantity in advance, because we had previously sold over 150,000 copies of his one-volume edition, Wells reduced his royalties on these sets to a mere fraction of his usual amount.

But we can't hope to sell any such quantity again. We can't risk manufacturing on any such huge scale as to bring our costs down to anywhere near the present low figures.

Of the 100,000 sets we contracted for, 95,000 have been sold. Less than 5,000 are left. And if you had seen the orders streaming in at a 500-a-day clip last season, you would realize how quickly these 5,000 sets will melt away.

While we still have books left, we want them to go to our own old customers and friends. We cannot, of course, discriminate against outsiders; we must fill the orders as they come in. But we can urge you to speak for your set now.

Here Is Our Offer.

Send the enclosed card—without money—and we will forward to you, post- paid, a set of Wells' "Outline of History" for a week's *Free Examination.* Open it up anywhere. Read a few pages. Then try to lay it down! If you don't find, as the *New York Tribune* put it, that "It's the most exciting book ever written," *send it back.* Scarcely one man in twenty has been willing to part with his set, once he's opened it!

The payments?—You will laugh at them! $1 a month for 12 months for this magnificent set of Wells', and a year's subscription to the *Review of Reviews* magazine.

You know the *Review of Reviews.* You know that it gives you the best that can be gotten in science, literature, drama, politics, philosophy and thought, in books, in international questions. In brief, it gives you all that is necessary to keep your mind alert and well-informed on the affairs of the day. It furnishes you the basis for sound conversation and clear thinking. It places you and keeps you among America's "Intellectual Aristocracy."

Not tomorrow, nor after lunch—for things to be done after lunch are frequently not done at all—but now, while this letter is before you, pencil your name and address on the enclosed card and drop it in the mail.

Then the orders may come and the books may go—by the hundreds—but you will be sure of your set by immediate prepaid shipment.

"It's been worth more to me than a College course," wrote one reader.

"If you can read but one book during the year," said President Hopkins of Dartmouth, "that book should be Wells' "Outline of History.""

The enclosed card brings it to you for a week—free.

———

WHY IS IT A TABLOID newspaper will outsell a clean, well-edited sheet by ten to one? Why? Because its appeal is to the sob sister, to the emotions. Why is it a Billy Sunday or an Aimee MacPherson can crowd great tabernacles, while your ordinary clergyman preaches to empty pews?

Emotion! The religion that brings masses of converts, that sweeps whole cities, is not an appeal to the intellect—but to the emotions! When Mohammed first preached his doctrines, they were sane and moderate—and they attracted few converts. He added the emotional features —*and swept over half the world!*

You may not be trying to start a new religion, but you do want action of some kind. And to get action, you need to arouse emotion on the part of your reader. You may convince his intellect that the thing you want him to do is right and is for his best advantage, but until you arouse in him an urgent desire to do it, until you make him feel that whatever effort it requires is of no account compared with the satisfaction it will bring him, your letter is lacking in its most important essential. It may have everything else, but if it lacks that faculty of arousing the right feeling, you might as well throw it away. It will never make you money.

Fifteen years ago there was a young fellow in a small Connecticut town with a book—and an idea. The book had been written for serious-minded men, to help show them the way to success. But letters and advertising telling of this marvelous secret of power had left their readers cold—so cold that the original publisher had failed. The young fellow had been his bookkeeper, and had bought the plates and stock at the sale of the publisher's effects.

You see, this young fellow had an idea he could sell that book. He believed that a mere description of its contents, such as had been used in the letters and ads, was not enough, that the important thing was to arouse the reader's desire through an appeal to his ambition. He had only $200 left, but he decided to gamble those $200 on selling the book.

To make a long story short, he did it. He spent his $200, and from them he got $2,000 worth of direct orders by mail! That $2,000 was the start of a small fortune. He promptly spent every cent of it in selling more books, pyramiding his receipts like a stock gambler does his winnings. In the fifteen years that have elapsed since then, that young man has sold more than $2,000,000 worth of books. His name is A. L. Pelton. The book was "Power of Will[1]." And he sold his two millions, as he did his two thousands, by making his appeal—not merely to the intellect, but to the emotions.

And his case is typical of every great mail success. What sold the "Book of Etiquette?" It had been gathering dust on the shelves of Doubleday, Page & Co.'s stock room for ten to fifteen years when Nelson Doubleday suddenly brought it to life and sold a million copies. What caused the sudden demand?

Not, you may be sure, any wave of culture or politeness sweeping over the nation, but simply the *fear* aroused in the readers of Doubleday's letters and advertisements that some unconscious gaucherie might cause them embarrassment.

---

1. https://archive.org/details/powerofwill00hadd

Why do people buy reducing belts, face creams, hair tonics? Why do they diet and go through arduous exercises? Not because their reason tells them they need these things, still less because they like them—but *because their emotion of vanity impels them!*

Appeal to the reason, by all means. Give people a logical excuse for buying that they can tell to their friends and use to salve their own consciences. But if you want to sell goods, if you want action of any kind, *base your real urge upon some primary emotion!*

Chapter 3 -
GETTING NEWS INTEREST INTO YOUR LETTER

WHAT THE WORLD WANTS, and has wanted since the beginning, is news— something to flag its jaded interest, something to stir its emotions.

Tell a man something new and you have his attention. Give it a personal twist or show its relation to his business and you have his interest.

Do you know how Wells' "Outline of History" was first put across? On its news value! "The Oldest Man in the World," "Was This the Flood of the Biblical Story" "The Finding of Moses," and so on. Newspaper headlines, all of them. News interest in every one of them. Rich man, poor man, beggar man, thief—all stop to read if you can put news interest into your letters.

"When the Rattlesnake Struck!" Can't you see yourself reading on to see what happened? Well, that is what thousands of others did every time that headline was used. It sold hundreds of thousands of O. Henry books.

"Will a Yellow King Rule the World ?" Which one of us would not be startled enough by such a headline to read on and see if there was any reason to fear that such a thing might ever really happen?

"What is the Unpardonable Sin in all Nature?" Can you imagine any reader so biased as not to go on at least a few lines further to find the answer to that question? And if you can lead him on those few lines, it is your own fault if you can not make your story so interesting that it

will carry him right down to the last line and the order blank or card that follows it.

A business man is no different from any other kind. Watch him on his way to the office. Compare the time he gives the financial and business news with the way he eagerly devours the details of the latest murder or scandal, or the attention he gives the "sports" page. He wants news interest. He will get it in his business as far as he can, but if it is not there, he will look outside his business for it.

So if you want his attention, go after it as the newspaper paragrapher does.

He knows he has to compete with a thousand other distractions, so he studies his reader and then presents first that side of his story most likely to attract the reader's interest.

You have to compete in the same way for your reader's attention. He is not looking for your letter. He has a thousand and one other things more important to him to occupy his mind. Why should he divert his attention from them to plow through pages of type about you or your projects?

You have, we shall assume, decided upon the emotion your letter must arouse in your reader to get him to do as you want. You know that every man is constantly holding a mental conversation with himself, the burden of which is his own interests—his business, his loved ones, his advancement.

And you have tried to chime in on that conversation with something that fits in with his thoughts. But some propositions do not lend themselves readily to this. What are you to do then? Look for news value! Look for something in or about your proposition of such news interest that it will divert the reader's mind temporarily from his own affairs, then bring it back by showing how your proposition fits in with those affairs or is necessary to their successful accomplishment. How are you to do it?

Perhaps the best way to explain that is to show a few examples of the way it has been successfully done. Here are some typical openings which get the reader's attention and lead logically on to a description of your proposition:

Do you know what was Socrates' chief characteristic? It was his pertinacious curiosity, his desire to know the why and the wherefore of everything, his questing for fundamental reasons.

It was this curiosity that helped make him represent the highest achievement of Greek civilization. It is that same questing for fundamentals that makes the Bland Advertising Agency so invaluable when a new product is to be introduced, a new field opened, and a new method tried.

———

IN THE CITY OF BAGHDAD lived Hakeem, the Wise One, and many there were who came to him for counsel, which he gave freely to all, asking nothing in return. One day there came to him a young man, who had spent much but got little, and asked: "Tell me, Wise One, what shall I do to receive the most for that which I spend?" Hakeem answered: "A thing that is bought or sold has no value unless it contains that which cannot be bought or sold. Look for the Priceless Ingredient."

"But what is this Priceless Ingredient?" persisted the young man. Spoke then the Wise One. "My son, the Priceless Ingredient of every product in the market place is the honor and integrity of him who made it. Consider his name before you buy."

For 25 years, Squibbs has been making, etc.

WHAT IS THE ETERNAL question which stands up and looks you and every sincere man squarely in the eye every morning?

"How can I better my condition?"

That is the real life question which confronts you, and will haunt you every day till you solve it. Read carefully the enclosed booklet, and see if you don't find in it the answer to this important life question which you and every man must solve if he expects ever to have more each Monday morning after pay day than he had the week before.

YOUR GRANDFATHER IN his buggy traveled no faster than Caesar; in individual transportation he was almost as limited as a citizen of Rome.

Suddenly—the automobile—and our generation is unshackled! With a car, miles shrivel up into minutes, and the humblest family leaves its doorstep to own the continent.

ALL DAY LONG, FROM the minute your mind takes the trail early in the morning, until you quit the game late at night—you are figuring on ways to sell more goods, to win more trade, to possess more executive ability, to be a bigger business builder.

This is the one great heart and soul aim of which you are ever conscious— the mastery of your business, the rising to supremacy in your line, the steady year in and year out increase of financial income. You'd willingly spend a few minutes to learn new ways of directing and developing your mental energies so as to cut out waste motion and make every move count for 100% progress.

Did you ever stop to think that the average man's brain wastes more energy than the worst old rattle-box that ever squandered good steam? It's the knowing how to apply your brain-power—how to think, how to reason, how to conserve mental energy, how to concentrate, that alone can make you a leader in your profession.

And it was to teach you how to think, how to concentrate, how to apply the basic fundamentals of all science to your own daily problems that the Blank Course was written. It shows you, etc.

IT WAS PAYDAY IN CONNELLSVILLE, Pa., and I was sitting in a local store, talking with the owner—When a laborer came in. He said he wanted so-and-so, that he, etc.

So I thought this: You want more business—want your store recognized as the, etc.

IF YOU ARE TIRED OF a salaried job, if you want to get into a big-paying, independent business of your own, I have a proposition that will interest you...

HERE'S A LITTLE "INSIDE information" that we're passing on to you, because you are a home-maker, and as such it concerns you.

We got a little low on summer stock the other day, so our buyer, Mr. Smith (he's full of ideas and enthusiasm) went to the source of supplies, and we just got a letter from him, thus: (Then give the news of some special buy that enables you to offer a wonderful bargain.)

WHAT IS IT WORTH TO keep baby's milk sweet? By making your refrigerator measure up to that all-important job, you make it measure up to all other jobs.

———

SOME TIME TODAY OR tomorrow or next month, in practically every commercial office in the U.S., an important executive will sit back in his chair and study a list of names on a sheet of white paper before him.

Your name may be on it. A position of responsibility is open, and he is face to face with the old, old problem—"Where can I find the man?" The faces, the words, the deeds, the possibilities of various employees pass through his mind in quick review, and he realizes once again how little an employer really knows about their hopes, their ambitions, their particular ability to handle more important work. That is where the Blank School can help him—and you.

———

WHAT HAS GIVEN THE high values to Iowa farm land? Corn. What has given the rapid advance in farm values to all the central western states? Corn. What is the biggest factor in making the farm lands of lower Louisiana advance?

Corn. Why? "Because they are in the corn belt."

———

IF YOUR EXPENSES WERE doubled tomorrow, could you meet them—without running heavily into debt? If you had to have more money on which to live—to support those dependent upon you—could you make it?

You could if you had the training afforded by our Course. It has doubled other men's salaries. It can do the same for you.

FOR 20 YEARS I WAS an exile, shunned by people on every hand, unwanted in the business world, impossible socially, a mental and physical wreck, a failure at everything. I was despondent, almost devoid of hope. Life to me was a burden.

And then I learned to talk! (And so on with description of a course to cure stammering.)

RIGHT AROUND NEW YEAR'S, most of us are somehow thinking about what we'll accomplish within the next twelve months. Often we get to figuring and planning and laying it all out beforehand.

So maybe it will mean a lot of inspiration to you, as it did to me, to read.

I HAVE COME TO LOOK upon it as a pity that circumstances should ever combine to place men of much ability in a position where they are not obliged to begin with a struggle for existence. For most individuals are so constituted that they are obliged to do so. The saving event in many a man's life is the blow that takes away the props that have supported him, and leaves him to look out for himself.

Many persons have told me that this is true of their own lives, and we know it is true of ours. So instead of railing against the fate that makes it necessary for you to dig in and make something of yourself, thank God for it, and start now getting ready. The Blank Course will fit you, etc.

The old gentleman who resigned from the Patent Office in 1886 because, as he said, everything had been invented, had nothing on the most of us. There are times when we all begin to feel that mechanical equipment is about as perfect as man can make it.

TAKE LUBRICATION FOR instance. In spite of the thousands of dollars wasted in furnishing six ounces of oil to a bearing that needs only one, production men are satisfied until, of course, someone comes along and shows them where 500% can be saved.

Making production men dissatisfied with their lubrication equipment is our business. Here is a new kind of Bolshevism that pays all around.

YOU'VE GOT TO HAVE more money. Your salary, without income, is not enough. The man who depends upon salary alone to make him rich, well-to- do or even comfortable, is making the mistake of his life. For the minute you stop working, the money stops coming in. Lose a day and you lose a day's pay—while expenses go right on.

Don't you think it's time you got Nature to work for you? A dollar put into a peach orchard will work for you days, nights and Sundays. It never stops to sleep or eat, but keeps on growing, growing—from the very minute you put your money in.

A SMALL MOSS LAMP IS sufficient to heat an Eskimo's igloo—because its walls are insulated. Minute particles of "dead air," held captive in the snow blocks, provide natural insulation—the most efficient known to science.

But present-day homes of ordinary construction waste two-thirds of the heat that comes from the furnaces.

One-third of this heat naturally escapes through windows and doors. The other third is unnecessarily wasted. It escapes easily through uninsulated walls and roofs.

Ordinary building materials cannot hold heat in. Celotex stops heat waste.

———

THERE'S A BANK HERE in Chicago—not much larger than yours—that secured over 280 new savings depositors last month! And secured them, mind you, on the sole strength of business-getting circular letters, without the aid of a single solicitor! That's why this letter is as vital to you as though it were a certified check. For it tells how, etc.

———

SUPPOSE A GOOD JOB were open where you work. Could you fill it? Could you jump right in and make good, or would the boss have to pass you up because you lacked training?

The man who is offered the big job is the man who has trained himself to hold it before it is offered to him.

Don't take chances on being promoted. Don't gamble on making good when your opportunity comes. If you want a big job that carries responsibility and

pays good money, get ready for it! Pick out the job you want in the work you like best. Then start right now to get, through the Blank Correspondence School, the training that will prepare you to hold it.

If you do as Arnold Bader did—he lives five miles north-east of Monticello—you will have very little trouble with your clover, and you can start a patch of alfalfa that will grow.

———

WHEN A MAN, 42 YEARS of age, who has been working for others all his life, decides to go into business for himself—and when, in a few short months, he so solidly establishes his business as to outdistance competitors who had the advantage of years of experience—there must be something about his method of doing business that other men would like to know about at once.

In the January magazine, you will find the story of how John Jones succeeded, what he did, etc.

———

PAY-DAY—WHAT DOES IT mean to you? Does your money go 'round? Or does it fail to stop all the gaps made by last week's or month's bills?

Last week according to actual, certified reports on file in our office—300 men got their salary raised as a direct result of becoming more proficient from studying ABC courses. Don't you think it's time that salary raise was coming your way?

———

THE OLD SAYING: "THERE is strength in numbers," certainly does not apply to the wearing apparel of the woman of today.

Could anything be more disappointing to a well dressed woman than to pass an exact counterpart of the coat which she is wearing, on some other woman?

Exclusiveness is the keynote of our women's coats; therefore we cannot permit any duplicates. That's the reason our Women's Coat Salon, etc.

"HOW'S THE GARDEN?—IS the morning greeting at the suburban station. Many estate owners are planting potatoes on all their available ground. Others, not so ambitious, are growing only enough for a table garden.

Under these conditions, House and Garden magazine assumes a new importance. It has already established a reputation for clear, usable garden information. Now, it is a guide book for the subject uppermost in everyone's mind.

YOU GET MORE PAY FOR each working hour now than you did the first day you worked. Why? Because you put more value into each hour of your time. You have developed your efficiency.

Your business efficiency grows out of your business ideas, and these come from your business knowledge. If you enrich your knowledge with the tested and proven experience of other men, you save yourself valuable time and the needless labor of studying out that which is already known. You add other men's business knowledge to your own efficiency. You get the material out of which to make new and original ideas.

It is these new ideas that make and break records. They mark the difference between the man who gets paid much and the one who receives little. And it is the material for these new ideas that you find in System, the Journal of Modern Business Management.

---

25 OR 30 YEARS AGO, back in the days when we traveled by the Dobbin and Dashboard route, men used to say—"Well, I reckon life insurance is a good thing, but you have to die to win.

Times have changed. And so have life insurance policies. Today there are at least 17 ways you can put life insurance to work for you, right now, in your own lifetime, and reap rich rewards without sacrificing the protection value of the policy.

No matter what business or personal undertaking you have in mind, there is probably a policy that will help you carry out the program easily, quickly, economically—and at the same time protect those dependent upon you.

Frankly, I'd like to discuss the matter with you, etc.

THERE IS ONE TYPE OF letter that is always interesting news, provided the product you are offering has an established market. That type is the price- reduction, money-saving offer. Here are a few such letters that have proved particularly effective:

Monday, March 6th—mark the date on your calendar now! It is the date of a sale you will not want to miss. A sale of women's white Spring frocks at $12.50. It is such an interesting event that we want to tell you a few things about it. Most of the dresses are, etc. At the close of a busy season, we find ourselves with 137 sets of the beautiful Gold Star edition of Oliver Cromwell's works slightly damaged from stock-room handling—so slightly you would have to make a close inspection to discern the damage, but still—you know how it is—they cannot be sold as perfect books.

So rather than send them back to the bindery and give the binders the profit of re-binding, we have decided to let the advantage go to a few booklovers—people like you who love good books for the books' sake and not for trifling details about them—and to offer these 137 sets at just what they would be worth with the covers ripped off!

AT CERTAIN PERIODS of the year, we have special events in this store which we do not advertise. In order that we may personally advise you of such sales, we would like to have your name and address. Won't you please therefore give us this information at the bottom of this card, and either send or bring it to the store at the first convenient opportunity?

ON THE 1ST OF OCTOBER, the rate of the Business Week will go up $1 a line. If you place your order before the 30th of this month, you can buy space to be used any time before January 1st at $—a line. After the 30th, positively no orders will be accepted at less than the new figure. As a matter of fact, our circulation entitles us to the higher rate now.

THAT ONE EXTRA DRESS you so badly wanted, but thoughtfully and economically decided not to buy—that smart afternoon frock, or the pretty street dress, that you longed for, but resisted because to buy it then would have been extravagant—is now, you will be happy to learn, turned into a matter of plain, common sense economy! For to make space for spring stock that is coming earlier than we were prepared for, we must cut the prices on our complete and beautiful line of winter styles to the point that will make it almost an extravagance not to take advantage of the wonderful values.

WE ARE ENCLOSING IN this envelope our check for $6.20 payable to Smith Bros. Readers. This means that if you endorse the check and return it to us before Dec. 10th, we will send you $6.20 worth of these readers, whichever ones you may choose! On the back of the check, you will find complete list of all our Readers, Grades 1A to 6B. If you wish to order additional quantities at this time, you can apply the enclosed check against our bill as part payment.

YOU WILL PROBABLY BE able to buy an Ever-ready Bag next year—10 years from now—But, you can never buy it again at its present price of $14.85.

That price is about to go up to $20. The special low payment, free-on-approval club is about to close for good.

This is your chance.

The card herewith brings the newest bag, etc.

OF COURSE, THERE ARE ways of flagging the reader's interest even before he gets to the first line of your letter. Putting a catch-phrase on the outside of the envelope is one. The *Literary Digest* employs this method on most of its mailings, so you can be sure they have found it effective, for no experienced user of the mails keeps up any practice that does not justify itself in increased orders on the record sheet.

As a rule, such catch-phrases on the outside of envelopes are effective only on third-class mail, to catch the reader's eye and arouse enough interest to get him to open your letter. The *Review of Reviews* has used them numbers of times to great advantage. In the O. Henry sale, they used such catch-lines as: "When the Rattlesnake Struck " "The Fateful

Kiss," "If This Happened on Your Wedding Night." In selling Simonds' "History of the World War," they had several that worked well, such as "And they said we wouldn't fight!" and "Retreat, H—l! We just got here!" Another, for a health course, was " 'If the damned fools only knew!' said Roosevelt."

All these helped to get the reader inside the envelope. Their purpose was the same as the newspaper headline—to arouse the reader's curiosity and make him go further into the story. So they have to be judged like any other headline, by the one standard—how successful are they in doing their job?

And the only way to find that out is to test them against other headlines, or against plain corner cards.

Even on third-class mail, we often find the plain corner cards better, and on first-class, it is almost invariably so. You see, the only object of a 2 cent stamp is to make the letter seem like a personal message, and to put a catch- phrase on the outside of the envelope defeats that object at once.

So a pretty safe rule to follow is—if you want to use an attention-getter on the outside of the envelope, save half your postage by sending your message third class.

One of the most effective stunts we have seen used to get a man to look inside the envelope was the idea of a young friend of ours. He watched trade papers, house organs and the like for pictures of men connected with different organizations. Then, instead of addressing the man by name, he pasted the man's picture on the front of the envelope and under it wrote: "Care of Such and Such a Company," and the address. It was subtly flattering and it won attention—favorable attention, too.

Folders often lend themselves to such attention-getting stunts even better than envelopes, for their size gives more room for illustration. In effect, they are advertisements sent through the mails, and they have to compete for their readers' interest in the same way as advertisements in a magazine. And their success or failure depends upon the same factors of attention-winning illustration and headline, interest-arousing start, clear description, logical argument and clincher, with coupon or card that makes ordering easy.

These are the more obvious ways of getting attention. Often they are so exaggerated that they defeat their own purpose. Quieter and usually more effective ways may be found in the letter itself, in the circular enclosure, or in the post card or order form.

Some offers lend themselves to a pictorial, colored letterhead. When Nelson Doubleday first offered his Little Nature Library, he used a plain letterhead.

By litho-graphing a nature scene of birds and woods and flowers across the top and down one side of his letterhead, he actually *doubled* the number of orders received from his letter! And the Little Leather Library increased their proportion of orders by almost as much.

On the other hand, we have seen numbers of offers which have pulled better results on a plain letterhead than on a colored, pictorial one. To be effective, pictures must not merely be attractively done—they must add essential background that would not be possible without them.

As an instance, at one time we offered a set of large gravure prints of famous pictures. By tipping in the upper left-hand comer of the letterhead a small reproduction of one of these prints, we added nearly 50 percent to the pulling power of the letter, and sold the prints (which had been gathering dust for years) at a goodly profit.

The same thing held true in selling calendars—a small reproduction in full colors of the picture we were using on the calendar, greatly increased the returns.

Where a business is built around some one personality, as in the case of Elbert Hubbard, his picture on the letterhead often adds 10, 15 or 20 percent to the pulling power of his letters. We found that to be so in testing different offers for John Blair, head of the New Process Company of Warren, Pa. And the same thing has been true of a number of people we have worked with.

Another effective attention-getter was to tip on the letterhead a sample of the product we were offering. When it was traveling bags, we gave a sample of the leather, to show how tough and long-wearing it was. When it was a topcoat or overcoat, we attached a sample of the cloth, so you could prove for yourself its wool content, see its attractive color and design, get the feel of it.

Then there is the fill-in, and the way the letter is folded, and the circulars and order card inserted. We frequently found that even so unimportant a thing as the fold made a difference in the orders. Folding the letterhead out, using the military fold so that only the salutation and first line of the letter showed when the reader picked it up, has increased orders for us at times by as much as 10 percent.

Indenting the main paragraph helps, too. We have found it a more effective way of calling attention to a special point of interest than either underlining or capitals.

Even the postage stamp has an effect upon the attention accorded a letter.

Two red 2 cent stamps pull more replies than one 4 cent stamp. One red 2 cent stamp pulls better than two green 1 cent stamps. A brown 1 1/2 cent stamp looks much like a 4 cent stamp, so it pulls better than a green 1 cent stamp, but no better than two 1/2 cent stamps!

As for the metered mail and postage indicia, experience varies, but in our own case, we have found postage stamps more effective than either.

To show what a difference color makes even here, we know at least one post office that permits the use of black ribbons in running 1 cent metered mail, and this 1 cent metered postage has frequently outpulled 2 cent stamp or meter!

These are minor details, of course, and not to be considered in the same breath with the start of the letter, the description, the argument or the close.

But when you have written a successful letter, when you have your appeal fight and are looking only for ways to get more orders, then you will be surprised at how these little minor details can make that order record mount!

Chapter 4 -
WORD PICTURES THAT MAKE PEOPLE WANT YOUR PRODUCT

NOW THAT YOU HAVE YOUR reader's interest, what are you going to do with it?

Start a series of firstly's, and secondly's and thirdly's, like the old-time Preacher, and put your reader to sleep, losing all the advantage you have worked so hard to gain? Go into a long-winded description that tires him out before he is halfway through? Or lead him gently from one point of interest to another, with word pictures so clear, so simple, that he can almost see the things you are offering him?

Getting your reader's attention is your first job. That done, your next problem is to put your idea across, to make him see it as you see it—in short, to visualize it so clearly that he can build it piece by piece in his own mind as a child builds a house of blocks, or puts together the pieces of a picture puzzle.

The mind thinks in pictures, you know. One good illustration is worth a thousand words. But one clear picture built up in the reader's mind by your words is worth a thousand drawings, for the reader colors that picture with his own imagination, which is more potent than all the brushes of all the world's artists.

And the secret of painting such a picture in the reader's mind is to take some familiar figure his mind can readily grasp, add one point of interest here, another there, and so on until you have built a complete word picture of what you have to offer. It is like building a house. You put up your framework. You add a roof, floors, sides, windows, doors, stairs, until you have your structure complete. You would not start with one side, or the roof. You get a solid foundation first; then you add to it logically, piece by piece, until you have your finished building.

Just so it is in building word pictures. Washington Irving gave a classic example of this in his description of the schoolmaster in "The Legend of Sleepy Hollow."

> *He was tall, but exceedingly lank, with narrow, sloping shoulders, long arms and legs, hands that dangled a mile out of his sleeves, and his whole framework most loosely hung together. His head was small...*

Can't you just picture that gawky, homely figure, with its ill-fitting clothes and shambling gait, the whole giving a scarecrow-like effect such as you see occasionally even today, where some youthful bumpkin seems to have sprouted so fast that arms and legs and Adam's apple have out distanced the rest of his anatomy in the race for development, until now they seem but a weak web holding together a bunch of limbs, with ham-like hands and arms at the ends.

Thousands of sales have been lost, millions of dollars worth of business have failed to materialize, solely because so few letter writers have that knack of visualizing a proposition—of painting it in words so the reader can see it as they see it.

Yet the ability to do that is perhaps the most important factor in a successful letter, for it means describing your proposition in terms of things the reader knows. Westcott gave a good example of this when he had David Harum tell some "horsey" friends about *The Lost Chord*.

> *It's about a feller sittin' one day by the organ, an' not feelin' exactly right—kind o' tired and out o' sorts and not knowing' jes' where he was drivin' at—jes' joggin' along with a loose rein*

for quite a piece, an' so on; an' then, by an by, strikin' fight into his gait and goin' on stronger and stronger, and fin'ly finishin' up with an A-aa-men that carries him quarter way 'round the track 'fore he can pull up.

You see, your sale must be made in your reader's mind. Before you can get his order, it is necessary for you to register a sequence of impressions in his mind, the combined result of which will be to make him want the thing you are offering more than the money or trouble it costs him. And the method of registering those impressions lies in first picking something with which he is familiar, and building on that.

To describe apples, for instance, as "like those with which Eve tempted Adam" is to use a simile that will strike a familiar chord with everyone. "Honey such as Cleopatra served to Antony," brings in another familiar allusion that almost anyone would recognize.

"As rich in appointment as Croesus in coin of the realm." "Satisfying as sinking a ten-foot putt on a rough green." "As much chance as a goldfish on a cat farm, " "Like a home run in the ninth inning with the bases full." "Like painting a battleship with a tooth brush" "Thick, creamy chocolate coatings that give you that 'moreish' feeling." "The company with a good product that does not advertise is like a man who whispers to himself on a desert." Every one of these stirs a familiar memory and thus gives you a definite impression to tie your story to. It is the difference between having foundation to build upon and resting your edifice upon shifting sands.

Further along in this book we shall give you numbers of instances of the way the writer has used this idea in describing various products he has helped to sell. Meantime, we give below a few go examples of how others have done it:

About a Ginger Ale

The lore which enters its making is akin to the lore of the wine-makers of France—a formula and process handed down from father to son. Only three men know the secret of its charm and vivacity, its mellow glow and friendliness. You will find in it stimulation like that of mountain air.

Silverware

The cheerful hum of voices, the steaming kettle, the cup that cheers, and Silver plate with its satiny surface catching every light.

A Room

It seemed, partly because the ceiling was low, to be very spacious; the walls and ceiling were of a kind of dusky amber hue; a golden brown was everywhere the prevailing tint. The tiny curtains, the long settees into which one sank, the chairs, the shades of the mellow glow lights—all were of some variety of this delicate, golden brown. In the middle of the room stood a square table.

A Rug

Under her feet a rug so thick that she felt her shoes must be hidden in its pile.

A Laundry

A goodly part of the delight of a dinner is in linen white as almond blossoms.

Napery, to be at its best, should be laundered carefully and skillfully. Many discerning housewives entrust their fine table linen to the White Laundry. In it, the constant thought is not "how quick" but "how well." But with all our care, we do save time for you, too.

A Book

If you are one of the live, wide-awake men who welcome the rush and tumult of great daring and big adventure, who believe that there is nothing better for tired brains or tired bodies than the healthy, blood-tingling, mind-quickening stimulation of a good story, then . . .

Hawaii

Four days beyond the Golden Gate, the Hawaiian Islands lift their crests of misty jade above a sparkling sea. Four nights away, the orange moon floods Moana Valley with its spell, and the ghosts of gorgeous flowers spread a witchery of perfume in the shadows. Four days away, the long combers, creaming on Waikiki's bar, race shoreward, and golden-skinned surf-riders, young gods and goddesses of the blue deep, speed across the amethystine waters.

Someone waits to drape a lei of jasmine on your shoulders. Someone waits to sing the husky croon, "Aloha oe," to echo in your heart for years. Why don't you go and capture your dreams?

A Ham

This mark certifies that the hog came from good stock, that it was corn-fed in order that it might be firm and sweet—that it was a barrow hog, so that the meat would be full-flavored and juicy—that it was a young hog, making the ham thin-skinned and tender—well-conditioned and fat, insuring the lean of the ham to be tasty and nutritious. This mark certifies that the ham was cured in sugar, pure saltpeter and only a very little salt, thus bringing out all the fine, rich, natural flavor of the carefully selected meat, and preserving it without "salty pickling."

A Real Estate Development

From every standpoint of the amusement industry and the real estate promoter, Boca Grande is a dead town. It always has been dead and probably always will be. That is why it appeals to many live people.

It doesn't quarrel with any of the bigger and better movements. It simply lets them alone. It has no Chamber of Commerce, no dredges or sand-suckers, and nothing proposed for 1931. Boca Grande is simply a haven for those who prefer to roll their own in the way of amusement. Providence did a perfectly satisfactory job in the way of making this a lovely place to swim and fish and golf, and we who have been wintering here since long before the boom came and went, let it go at that.

You might like Boca Grande a lot. Many clever people do. It is an adventure in naturalness. Let us send you a book about it. It is a very nice book, and not too much exaggerated.

An Electric Refrigerator

Just a few degrees below the temperature of an ordinary ice-box is a colder zone that affects the keeping of foods in a remarkable way. It is the zone where moisture crystallizes out of the air as frost, leaving the air dry, crisp and snappy. At this lower temperature, the air takes on a frosty sting. This is the zone of So-and-so, produced by So-and-so electric refrigeration.

A Gas Burner

The Blank Heat-Spreading Burner is a nest of small jets, and is so designed that the heat is spread evenly over the entire bottom of the utensil. Combustion is so perfect that all the fuel is burned. You get the full benefit of every atom of gas.

The bottom of the cooking utensil rests only seven-eighths of an inch from the burner top. There are no deposits of carbon to be scoured off.

An Oven

This is the Blank Oven, built on the principle of the Dutch oven, with the "baker's arch" to prevent air pockets. The patented heat spreader at the bottom assures even distribution of heat, and guards against your roasts and baked things being underdone on top and burnt on the bottom. On the door of the oven there is a heat indicator which shows how much heat there is inside.

And here are a few from England which tend to show that our cousins across the water are not as deficient in humor as the "funny papers" would lead us to believe. Certainly their descriptions would be hard to improve upon.

A Plum Cake

It was in one of those sweet old country houses where they put little bunches of lavender with the linen that we first tasted the plum cake of our dreams— glorious stuff, rich, fragrant and incredibly plummy. We admit now that our mouth was too full when we asked for the recipe, but we were overwrought and excited; anyhow, let bygones be bygones, they gave us the recipe for our customers.

The dear old housekeeper, with her ringlets and black taffeta, took us to the still room to show us how to make it, and told us fascinating things; how brown- shelled eggs are best, and how it is most auspicious to make such a cake when the moon is in its second quarter. That is why you so often see our chef on our roof in Piccadilly anxiously scanning the heavens on fine nights.

Turtle Soup

When we speak of turtle soup, our voice becomes very tender—do not think us unmanly. We have in mind the spiced turtle soup we make for those who feast regally. As you gaze into its depths, you see luscious calipee and morsels of calipash gleaming darkly through the soup that is so rich and yet so wondrous clear. Then there is our special turtle soup, cleared of all heaviness and fat, that brings roses back to the cheeks of delicate people.

Once a rival, maddened by jealousy, came and spoke lightly of our turtle soup. We killed him. It was wrong of us, for we held no game license that season, but it shows we are not unmanly.

Cakes

We have these cakes made at a little rose-covered country house, by people steeped in the sweet lore of home-made cake-craft. We will not even let them come to London for a holiday, for fear they should be contaminated by modern methods. So there they abide, unhurried and at peace, with bowls of rose water at their elbows, and little sprigs of rosemary and great crocks of buttermilk, making glorious cakes full of the goodness that is England.

Could such cakes as these be made within earshot of a London motor-bus? We think not.

A Cheese

There is in England one incomparable herd of glossy little Guernsey cows that give milk that is about one-third cream. It is from this wonderful herd that we obtain our butter. That is why there is no mistaking its golden churn.

With all humility, we say there are few, if any, cheeses as good as ours to be obtained in England. For many years we have obtained them from the same prize dairy.

We have kept a few of last year's Cheddars for those who love the ripe splendour of well matured cheese.

Do not be misguided by the mirthless Stiltons made in hissing factories by pale youths who cycle madly to the cinema when freedom hoots from the powerhouse.

Our real farm-house Stiltons will show you why the name is venerated by mankind. Each cheese is made in the homestead of a Leicestershire yeoman, from great pans of cream, and aprons full of cowslips for the coloring. When such cheeses as these enter the dining rooms; of clubs, the faces of brigadiers soften, and admirals give little plaintive cries of love.

Chinese Ginger

Fat-root ginger with its generous warmth curbed by sweetness. And then there is the syrup—lazy in its richness.

Ham

Deep-sheathed in ivory-white fat, and close set with rosy meat...

The eating of them makes a man realize how fond he is of all his relatives — well, practically all.

Bacon

When the fragrance of its frying rises through the area, passers-by give savage cries and raven at the railings. This is one of the disadvantages of living in town.

The fascination of our bacon lies in the secret manner of its curing. It is mellowed in the suave smoke of certain rare woods and old-world herbs. Bacon with meaning and beauty in every mouthful. Often we stand for hours before a side of our wonderful bacon, musing in deep reverie, and finding therein our greatest happiness.

Put life into your descriptions—life, and when possible, a smile. Give your reader something that will stir him out of his indifference, arouse his emotions.

You never see "Standing Room Only!" signs in front of an art museum or a public library or a theater where educational films or travelogues are being shown. But just try to get into almost any good movie around eight o'clock of an evening! Why the difference?

Because most people cultivate their intellects only under the lash. They revel in emotion at any and all times.

So give them a thrill! If you want to describe your mustard, weave it into a story. Tell how the girl planned this picnic lunch; of the loving care that went into every bit of it; the touch of this; the flavor of that; the delicious ham; the savory mustard; and then how the boy forgot them all just in the delight of being with her.

Tell about the man so poor he did not have a penny even to buy his boy the velocipede he had been begging Santa to bring him; so after the little tot had gone to bed, Dad sat down with his pocket knife and some old lumber and carved out a sort of wooden velocipede that not only delighted the boy's heart, but when shown to a toy manufacturer, put Daddy beyond the reach of want for the rest of his days.

Tell how the rubber tire owed its inception to the efforts of a young veterinary to make a more comfortable wheelchair for his invalid mother; how the first mowing machine consisted of a number of scissors with one side nailed to a board, the other connected to a string which opened and shut them. Get the story back of your product. Give your reader a laugh or a tear or a lump in his throat. Stir up his emotions! You will have no trouble interesting him then!

Compare the following advertisements, for instance. The first three are good ads and pulled a reasonable number of orders. They were successful, as advertisements go. But their appeal was solely to the intellect. Once we had tried the style outlined in the last four ads, we discarded the other kind entirely, for the emotional type tripled and quadrupled our returns.

No. 1.

Roosevelt said, "Mr. Frank H. Simonds' "History of the Great War" is a very remarkable work, and I look forward eagerly to the appearance of the remaining volumes. It is not too much to say that no other man in this or any other country can quite parallel the work that Mr. Simonds has done. It is hard to say what most to admire; the really extraordinary grasp of the essential facts of the war which is shown; or the transparent clearness with which the facts are brought out; or the entire fairness and impartiality of the conclusions."

No. 2.

Colleges Study This History Yale

University has ordered 400 copies of selected chapters from Simonds' "History of the World War" for use as a textbook in its history classes. Ex-President Hadley says of it: "I have had so much pleasure from what Simonds has already written about the war that I shall be particularly glad to have the results of his observations and conclusions in a more permanent form."

Once in a generation, perhaps, there appears a man with the gift for making history vital, alive, interesting—a man like Ridpath or Macaulay—a genius that combines a natural gift for language, a natural gift for history and a natural gift for facts with great vision and the ability to make you see and be thrilled by his vision.

Frank H. Simonds is this generation's Ridpath—this war's Macaulay. His tale is simple and direct enough to captivate children, yet so profoundly true as to hold the greatest scholar.

No. 3.

Ever since the day in July, 1914, when one flaming editorial of his startled the world with its prophecy of the great war, Simonds has been the one pre-eminent writer on the war. He is quoted by newspapers the world over. The British Government has had his articles reprinted and distributed broadcast.

The French Government has conferred upon him alone of all the Historians of the war the Cross of the Chevalier of the Legion of Honor. The Greek Government has made him an Officer of the Royal Order of the Redeemer. The King of Rumania has named him an Officer of the Royal Order of the Star of Rumania.

To no other writer did statesmen and generals so freely and frankly give information. No other military critic was so often quoted or so highly regarded as an authority. Multitudes based their opinions upon his judgment. His words governed the hopes and fears of millions.

So it is wonderful indeed that you can now have the whole story of the war in its final form written by him, with interesting special articles and illuminating sidelights by the greatest military, naval, and political leaders of America and Europe.

No. 4.

"My right has been driven in, my left has been driven in—consequently with all that is left of my center, I will now attack." —Foch.

That is the terse report that General Foch sent to Joffre at the crucial moment of the battle of the Marne. Told that his troops were worn out by the three days of continuous fighting—Too Tired?" he cried. "So are the Germans. Attack!" And attack they did in gallant style. He drew together all his exhausted divisions, all his reserves, and at the very moment when the enemy thought him routed, he smashed against the Prussian Guard in a violent, desperate assault, broke through its lines, crushed them and saved Paris!

How Much Do You Know of This Brilliant Leader?

Do you know that he is everywhere considered one of the greatest tacticians the

world has known? Do you know that it was he who saved the channel ports of Calais and Dunkirk, and thus made possible the uninterrupted passage of men and supplies from England? Do you know that he was the man who took in hand the Italian defense just at the moment the Austro-German drive was at its height, and not only saved Venice, but changed almost certain defeat into glorious victory?

The History of the Great War Gives a detailed account of these exploits as well as the whole story of the war.

You read in it of the heroic stand, etc.

No. 5.

A Rude Awakening

(The illustration for this ad showed the

Kaiser seated, with a huge firecracker

labeled "A.E.F." just ready to go off behind him.)

The Kaiser has again and again assured his people they have nothing to fear from America—that all we shall ever be able to get past his U-boats is a few divisions of troops and some shiploads of supplies—that the tales of huge armies being formed, of mountains of munitions being manufactured, of flocks of airplanes and great fleets of ships, are just "American bluff."

What a Rude Awakening Is in Store for Him

Already our men are in the battle line by the hundred thousand; already our Navy has definitely checked the U-boat menace. Soon we shall have more than a million men in France and two million more are in training, and our shipbuilding alone will more than replace any future losses from submarines and mines.

But to definitely defeat the German Military Power, to win the war and make the world safe for the next hundred years, will take every bit of energy, every ounce of force that we can muster; and one of the first things necessary to get the most out of our enormous resources is to know all about the war—what led up to it, how it began, through it all. Where can you find all this? In, etc.

No. 6.

The Terrible Year

This, according to the German plan, was to be "The Terrible Year." The German High Command realized the necessity of getting a decision before the full American strength could make itself felt, so their strategy was to keep hammering the Allies until they had pounded their way through to Paris or the English Channel, and forced the Allies to accept a German peace.

But the Americans Turned the Tide Against all the German expectations, America solved her transport problem so speedily, so successfully, that she was able to pour men into the fighting by the hundred thousand right at the crucial moment, turning German victory into overwhelming disaster.

Not only did Our Boys stop the German and hurl the Prussian hordes back over the Marne, but it was their energy and dash that enabled Foch to counterdrive so successfully, capturing thousands of prisoners and literally mountains of munitions.

The History of the World War gives you in vivid, pulsing narrative, etc.

No. 7.

The Coming of the Yanks

The battle of Chateau-Thiery was at its height. The Germans were pouring in such a hurricane of shot and shell, liquid fire and poison gas that the French Poilus, staunch veterans though they were, had begun to give way before that storm of destruction, and the never-ending hordes of on-rushing Huns.

Already the French Commander was preparing for a hurried retreat. Already he had ordered his hospital, with its hundreds of wounded, moved to the rear. The outlook was dark indeed—the road to Paris and the heart of France seemed open to the invader, when suddenly from over the hill behind the French lines came the sound of martial music—of thousands of fresh young voices singing—singing cheerily, confidently, exultantly—

The Yanks are coming,

The Yanks are coming,

The Yanks are coming over there!

And through the mist and battle smoke broke the long lines of Americans, their guns at the charge, their bayonets fixed, every man singing—exultant at the chance to get at the foe.

They went at the Germans like so many wild-cats. They killed them with bayonet, with rifle butt or with knife. They charged right into the face of machine guns—tore them apart—choked the gunners with bare hands! In two short, glorious hours, the whole war was won.

In two hours that will rank in history with Waterloo or Gettysburg, the Germans woke to the fact that they had not a chance—that they were fighting against something too big for them to meet—a spirit so high that no force of theirs could stop it.

The full story of Chateau Thierry has never been written. Not in any newspaper or magazine can you find the things our boys did that day. It is only around some confidential table where men high in the counsels of our Allies meet that the truth is freely told.

But now at last you can know the full story of that wonderful battle—of how our boys brought it home to the Germans that the end had come. It is a stupendous story. It will make every American heart beat faster. You can read it, just as it really happened, in

Simonds' "History of the World War."

Chapter 5 -
MOTIVES THAT MAKE PEOPLE BUY

MOST PEOPLE ARE LIKE automobiles. They can be pushed or pulled along, or they can be moved to action by starting their own motive power from within. In either case, you must provide the fuel. And the only fuel that will start the sort of action you want from within is *desire.* Arousing that desire in your reader is known as the gentle art of exercising persuasion.

What is persuasion? Nothing but finding the motive that will impel your reader to do as you wish, then stirring it to the point where it is stronger than his inertia, or his economical tendencies.

To do that, you must show how he is going to benefit, and you can not do it unless you have the faculty of putting yourself in his place. Would you be richer, healthier, happier for having done the thing you ask? Would it help your standing with others? Would it enable you to do anything, write anything, say anything better than you could before? Is it something everyone should have?

Would it gratify any passion? Would it enable you to help those you love?

Would it prevent loss of money or the respect of others?

Only the new letter-writer selects the arguments that are nearest to hand—the viewpoints that appeal to his own selfish interests. The experienced writer asks himself such questions as those above, then picks the motive that is strongest and presents it from the viewpoint of the reader alone. He shows what it will do for the reader, what it will add to his prestige, to his power, to his comfort, to the wellbeing of those he loves.

Description of your product is necessary. But description, no matter how interestingly done, will never sell your product by the thousands. It is what it will do for the one who buys it that counts! There are six prime motives of human action: love, gain, duty, pride, self—indulgence and self—preservation. And frequently they are so mixed together that it is hard to tell which to work on more strongly. A man may want a new car, for instance, solely from a feeling of pride in its fine appearance, but unless money is a matter of no moment to him, pride alone will seldom make him buy.

To make that pride motive so strong as to sweep caution to the winds, you must reinforce it with a touch of self-indulgence, a measure of love and duty for wife and family, and a large dash of gain. Show how the old car hurts his standing, how repair bills and higher gas and oil consumption eat into the difference in price, how he can effect some saving now that will not be possible a month or a year later.

The more motives you can appeal to, of course, the more successful you will be, but it is important that you differentiate between the motive that makes him desire a thing and the one that impels him to take the action you desire, for the whole purpose of your letter is to make your reader act as you wish him to. He may not want to pay a bill, for instance. He may need the money badly for himself, and all his inclinations may be towards keeping it in his pocket. But if you can "sell" him the idea that his credit means more to him than the possession of that money or anything it can buy him, you have touched the right motive.

What has he to gain by doing as you wish? What to lose by refusing? "If someone were to make your boy a thief," read a National Cash Register

Company letter. "Feeling as you do about your own boy, is it right to put temptation in the way of other men's boys?

Love and pride and duty are all intermingled there, with the added inducement of gain implied—of saving the losses from petty thefts and the like. But love is the dominant motive.

Love is always the strongest motive. You have but to read the papers to see how men are every day giving everything they have for it—riches and honor, life itself. Yet love is one of the most difficult motives to effectively work into a letter. Because it is so universal, it has been harped upon to such an extent that the letter writer has to be more adroit in its use than with any other motive.

Gain, now; that is easy. True, it has been worked to death, too, but we are a gullible race, and we are much readier to believe that someone is unselfishly interested in helping us to make or save money, than that he will go out of his way to further the well-being of those near and dear to us.

Tell a man, for instance, that you have only two cars left in stock, or ten suits in his size, or a hundred sets of books, and when the new stock comes in the price will be advanced 25 percent, but since he is an old customer you are holding one of these for him at the old price, and he will believe you. But try to tell the same man that your only reason for trying to sell the "Book of Knowledge" or the "Junior Classics" is your ardent love for and interest in the well-being of children, and he will laugh at you. He may buy these books if the good they will do his children is adroitly presented to him, but he resents having his love for them used as a leverage to dig money out of him for you.

Here is a skillful appeal to pride that was used with great success in the days before the automobile had crowded the horse and buggy off the road, and that can still be adapted to many another product just as successfully:

Mr. John Jones,

Jonesboro, N. C.

DEAR SIR:

Mr. Smith, our factory manager, just came in with your inquiry of Jan. 1st. He read it to me and said:

"You remember Mr. Jones, don't you? He stands pretty high over there in Jonesboro where he lives—lots of folks know him. If Mr. Jones could drive one of our buggies around and tell his friends and neighbors who made it and how well satisfied he is with it, we could sell a lot more buggies in that neighborhood this coming year."

Then he suggested an idea which I know will please you immensely, Mr. Jones. Here it is:

I am having made to order for my own personal use just about the finest buggy that money can buy. Here's a blueprint of it. See the extra strength I've built into the wheels. Note the triple ply springs that make riding easier. Mr. Smith just said: "Mr. Jones would surely be delighted with a buggy like yours. Why don't you offer him this one? You can make another for yourself."

He thinks that if I send you my built-to-order buggy, you as a man who knows buggies, who knows what materials and finish ought to go into good buggies, will surely be pleased with it and certainly be envied by friends and acquaintances of yours who will see and admire my buggy when you drive it. I know Smith is right. So I've decided to act on his suggestion and let you have the buggy I've taken such great personal pride in designing.

Now, Mr. Jones, if an extra-fine buggy—one built specially to order for the President of the Columbus Buggy Co. would interest you—if such a buggy, with its longer wear and smarter appearance, would be worth a few dollars more to you—if you'd like to drive a buggy you'll be proud of all your life, just fill out the attached form, send it back by return mail, and I'll ship you a buggy like mine at once, or if you say so, I'll send you the buggy now being made for me, and make another one for myself.

OF COURSE, CLOTHES don't make the man. But you know yourself how helpful they are in getting him a hearing.

It is likely that Tom Edison or Charlie Schwab could wear any kind of clothes and not suffer particular loss of prestige if the suit happened to be shabby or a misfit.

But most of us have to be a bit mom careful. Aside from what our friends might think of us, we don't feel right ourselves unless we have the consciousness of being well-groomed.

THROUGH A FORTUNATE purchase of fine wool, we are able to offer this MacCarden Motor Robe at a special low price of $9.85—about $5 or $6 less than you would expect to pay for a good robe in a retail store. We have been notified, however, that future wool will cost us much more; and we cannot hope to continue the $9.85 price when our present supply is gone.

Just glance over the enclosed folder and think for one moment of the absorbing, fascinating story that goes with it—education in the highest sense, entertain- ment in the most educational sense. People who have read this new, finally revised edition of the Outline are saying that it has done more for them than a College education. A College education costs you probably $5,000 and four years of your life. Wells' wonderful work is sent to you on approval, and you will read the four books as absorbedly, as quickly as so many novels.

ONE OF THE OLDEST FIRMS in the rubber business—a factory which makes tires that are as good as any in the world—wants to see if car owners will buy their tires 'direct' if he will sell to them at just about the price dealers now pay.

This tire manufacturer knows that such a saving can be made if a lot of unnecessary selling expense and middlemen's profits are wiped out. So he's going to test out the motoring public by offering the very best tires he makes direct to car owners through our selling organization which operates by mail all over the country.

And to quickly find out if men really want to save 25% on the best tires that can be made, he is having us rush out this August letter to a few selected car owners.

WE HAVE JUST 790 OF these double-texture, all wool Great coats to sell at this low price. When they are gone, your chance to save on your Winter Ulster will go with them. But while these 790 last, you can get as perfect-fitting, as good- looking, as fine-quality a Winter Overcoat as ever you would want to wear, at an almost unheard-of bargain.

As Resident Buyers for a number of out-of-town stores, we are making the rounds of the manufacturers every day, and whenever they bring out some "special," whenever they close out some small lot, whenever they finish copying some designer's model-gown, *we get it!*

You know yourself what bargains you can pick up even in the stores just by shopping around. Imagine, then, what we can do when we are daily shopping among the manufacturer's themselves. A fourth off, a third off, even a half off the regular wholesale price is nothing unusual, for manufacturer's have no time to bother with these small lots, and they give them to us at practically our own price.

The result is that we can offer you some of the season's loveliest and most distinctive models, in all sizes, in the most fashionable colors and materials, *at actually less than their regular wholesale prices!*

NEARLY EVERY MAN CAN look back—and not so far back with most of us—and recall cases where some little slip lost him opportunity or prestige, cost him the favor of someone whose good opinion he valued, turned what might have been a valuable friendship into enmity or indifference.

But there is no need to lose more such opportunities. For just as a physician may read medicine, just as a lawyer may read law, just so may you now read the science of culture—that science of good breeding which includes etiquette but yet is above and beyond all etiquette.

One of the best opportunities for the use of persuasion is in collection letters.

As a matter of fact, it is our opinion that there are only two ways to collect old accounts. The first is persuasion. The second is the threat of court action or loss of credit standing.

Our own idea is that the most effective collection series is one that alternates these two. When you send out a strong threat you frighten a certain number of delinquents into paying, but you make the others so mad they swear they will never pay. Send another threat on top of that and you just make them madder.

But use persuasion and you smooth down their fur, get a number of payments, and have things all set for another effective threat.

Here are a few samples of persuasive collection letters:

You remember how Abraham Lincoln walked many weary miles from the grocery store where he earned a mere pittance, in order to bring to a poor old woman the few cents change she had forgotten and left on the counter.

And how Mark Twain, because his name happened to be associated with that of an unsuccessful company, took all its heavy debts upon himself, and, though an old man, paid every one.

It is this "I-will-owe-no-man-a-penny" spirit that builds up and strengthens self-respect and personal integrity—and makes a credit reputation that bulwarks a man in time of need. It is because we find just such good old-fashioned honesty as this in 99% of the folks with whom we do business, that we feel sure of the payment of your account, even though it has been neglected recently.

UNLESS YOU HAVE CONDUCTED a similar business, you can hardly conceive of the mass of detail involved in handling many thousands of these $1 and $2 accounts. The difference between profit and loss on such a business depends upon the promptness of collections more than on any other one thing. I know you will not consciously be instrumental in working a hardship on any concern with which you do business, and I am quite sure that when you see your failure to remit promptly is doing just that, you will send me a check by return mail.

Back in the Stone Age, records were carved on a stone slab. When the debt was due, Mr. Creditor presented the account in a very polite fashion—holding the slab in one hand while in the other he carried his stone mallet. The debtor had no alternative.

Then civilization moved on until the debtor's prison was the deciding factor as to whether a debtor would pay or not. But now it is a different proposition— credit. Every kind of business, large or small, must build its foundation on its credit standing. Concerns liquidating their obligations at maturity build their credit standing to the highest point attainable, while those who allow their obligations to run along month after month without payment, decrease their credit standing until it is nearly obliterated.

Again, as perhaps in your case, there is the business man who is too busy with matters of more importance, and the work of looking after his financial and accounting details is delegated to some other person who lets these important factors ride without considering the detrimental effect they have on your credit standing.

YOUR NAME IN RED INK on our records is something we want to avoid. You do, too, I am sure. Here is the way the account now stands:

John Johnson—Bills Receivable—$25.00

But unless we receive a check by the 17th, here is the way our book-keeping department will have to enter it.

(Red Ink) John Johnson—Account Overdue $25.00

The bad feature about this entry is the effect it has on our credit man, and the credit men of all the other stores that belong to our Association. But then your check before the 17th prevents all this.

THE RECORDS IN THE case show that your account has been PAST DUE for 90 days, and that you have failed to return the goods or make payment, or to advise the Blank Company of cause for delay. The records also show that though written repeatedly, you have shown no inclination to liquidate your indebtedness. You have COMPELLED them to turn the account over to the Legal Department to take such action as may protect the interests of the company.

That you may be fully cognizant of the law, I wish to advise you that obtaining goods with an intent to defraud constitutes a criminal act and if such fraud is proved, the person committing it is liable to imprisonment.

Your case is now on the records of the Legal Department, and will come up for attention in one week unless you make remittance to the Blank Company.

It is to be hoped you will, for your own protection, make payment if you desire to avoid the annoyance, publicity and cost of a lawsuit. You remember a famous English Jurist is reported to have said that if a man claimed the coat on his back, and threatened to sue him for it, he'd give him the coat rather than risk losing his waistcoat, too, in defending the lawsuit.

If that is true when you are in the right, how much more true it must be when the facts are so strongly against you as in the present case!

Summed up, arousing the right motive comes down to making the reader want what you have to offer, whether that be merchandise or money or credit or merely a clean bill of health—not merely for what it is, but for what it will do for him!

When you can get him thinking along those lines, when you can bring home to him the advantages that will accrue to him from doing as you wish, in so effective a way that he wants these more than anything or any trouble they may cost him, then you can feel that you have demonstrated the gentle art of exercising persuasion.

Chapter 6 -
THE PROOF OF THE PUDDING

OUT IN A LITTLE TOWN in northwestern Pennsylvania is a mail order house which built a business from scratch, to over a million dollars a year on one basis only—proof.

They described their products to the best of their ability, they followed the usual rules of attention and interest, but for their main argument they used proof.

One of their most effective letters read:

> *When 10,000 men from all over the country send all the way out here just to get a raincoat, there must be something unusual about these coats. And when a man like John Jones of such and such a street in your town [and here they gave the name of an actual buyer in the town, frequently a man whose name was well known] not only sends for a Blank Coat, but is so well pleased with it that he writes: "Your Blank Coat is not only the finest quality and the best fit I have had in a coat for a long time, but an unusual value. I haven't been able to find its equal in our local stores at twice the price."*
>
> *When thousands of well-dressed business and professional men from all over the country write us letters like that, and when more than a dozen of your own fellow townsmen have sent for this same coat, and liked it so well that they gladly sent up $14.65 for it and felt that they were saving $ 10 to $15 each when they did it—don't you think it would be worth your while to at least look at so unusual a value, especially when the*

enclosed card will bring one to you in your exact size without one penny of cost or one bit of obligation?

In the beginning, of course, it was more difficult. They had no ten thousand customers to refer to. So at the start they depended for their proof upon the "free-examination, no-money-until-you-have-tried-it-for-a-week-plan." That helped to establish confidence. And as fast as they got an order they did their utmost to turn it into a satisfied customer from whom they could get a testimonial. The testimonials were bait, and with them they tempted every man in the town or state where the writer lived.

That the idea was sound was proved by the results. Tucked away off in a comer of Pennsylvania, in a town no one had ever heard of, without capital, without special advantages of any kind, they built their business to a volume of over a million dollars. Why? Because statements which, coming from themselves, would have been laughed at, were accepted at face value when they came from the mouths of their customers.

Perhaps even this alone might not have been convincing had they not backed up these statements with the "free-examination, no-money-until-you-have-tried-it-for-a-week' idea, which showed that they not only believed the statements to be true, but had every confidence in the ability of the goods to back them up.

Every sales letter must have argument or proof of some kind, but all the argument in the world is not equal to proof such as this:

"You know Jim Jones, who lives over on Vesey Street, a few blocks from you. Here is what he says...

But we don't ask you to take his word for it. We don't ask you to believe even such men as this Senator, and that Congressman, and a nationally known banker or lawyer or whatnot.

*Try it for yourself and see! The enclosed card brings it to you
without cost and without obligation, for a week's free try out."*

What is it that sells patent medicines by the millions every year? What is it that makes men swallow gallons of nasty, unpalatable nostrums, pounds of seaweed, and yeast cakes put up in all manner of forms? Proof! A man describes your symptoms with such exactitude that you think he must have taken a look down your epiglottis, then assures you that one dose or a dozen pills or cakes of yeast relieved him of every trace of his ailment.

What is there for you to do but to try some of the same? If the remedy was so efficacious with him, you naturally reason it will not do any harm to try a little of it yourself. And so the sales go on.

We are a credulous people, but we have become so accustomed to hearing every one claim that his product is the best in the world, or the cheapest, that we take all such statements with a grain of salt. Let some third person make the statement, however, apparently from excess of enthusiasm over the wonderful value or service he has received, and we prick up our ears. Let that be backed by positive proof and we are ready to risk our money.

For that reason, it usually pays to put a testimonial into every letter you write. I know one unusually successful mail order man who will not let even a collection letter go out of his house without a testimonial in it. And I believe he is right. For why doesn't your customer pay his bill? Frequently because he is not satisfied with your product, not quite sold on the idea that it is as good value for the money as he had expected. More than anyone else, he needs to be convinced of this, and what surer way to convince him than through the mouth of some one who has used it?

True, testimonials are in rather bad odor of late, due to the way advertisers have run after celebrities and bought their endorsement of everything from chewing gum to pajamas. But there never will be a time when a testimonial, which has the ring of truth about it, will not be a potent factor in dispelling doubt in the mind of a hesitant customer.

Chapter 7 -
SUPPLYING THAT IMPULSE

WATCH THE CROWD IN front of a sideshow. At just the critical moment in the barker's talk, his assistants on the outside of the crowd start a general push forward towards the ticket window.

In every sale, whether in person or by mail, there comes that same critical moment. Your prospective customer is almost convinced.

You have his attention, you have aroused his interest, you have just about persuaded him that he must have the thing you are offering, you have proved to him beyond question that it is the best or the cheapest; but he is not quite ready to sign on the dotted line. Caution, inertia, call it what you will, urges him to hold back.

Desire, the appeal of a bargain, is goading him on. He is hesitating, teetering, first this way and then that. Too much urging will make him draw back. Too little will leave him where he is. What are you to do?

Give him a push without seeming to do so. Like the circus barker's assistants, supply the impulse that will make it easier for him to go forward with the crowd than to stand still or draw back. How are you to do it?

You already know the motive it is necessary to arouse to make your sale, so look for some easy preliminary task on which you can set that motive busy.

Then see if you can make it easier for your customer, already started, to keep going forward rather than stop and turn around and go back.

In personal selling you find examples of this every day. What does an automobile advertisement try to make you do! Buy a car? Not at all. "Come and look at our beautiful new models"—that's all. "No obligation whatever. It will be a pleasure to show them to you."

You go, and what happens? Does the salesman urge you to buy? No, indeed! He shows you around most readily, notes the car you like, gets you to sit in it, to feel the clutch, to sense all the comfort and luxury of it. Then he asks if you would like to drive it out to the country next Sunday "Just to see how beautifully it runs."

He has it in front of your house at the appointed time or a little before. He gives up the driver's seat to you at once. He says nothing about a sale just calls your attention to the gentle purr of the motor, to the way it breasts the hills, to this little comfort and that knickknack. And when he gets you back to your door, he gently insinuates: "Now, what time shall I send it around tomorrow," or "Well, let's take a look at the old car now, and see how much we could allow on it." And almost before you know it, you have a new car.

That is salesmanship. And that is the sort of salesmanship you must put into every letter. Just remember that nearly every man balks at making a decision that is going to cost him money. He wants time to think it over. He hates to commit himself definitely.

So humor him. Tell him frankly: "Don't decide now. Plenty of time for that later. Just fill in your height, your weight and your collar size on the enclosed card, and we'll send you a Keep dry Coat in your exact size. Try it out. Wear it for a week. Take it down town and compare it with anything you can find in your local stores. *Then* decide."

Don't you see how much easier that is? Nothing to worry about, no decision to make—just take a look at the coat when it comes. If it fits nicely and you like it, wear it down town and compare it for value with coats in the stores there.

After all, there is nothing final about it. If you change your mind, you can easily send it back.

But when the coat comes, what happens! You may be away, or the weather is warm, so you do not wear it. And it lies around the house for a week or two.

Then along comes a bill. My, you will have to get at that coat and try it! You get it out. You are reasonably well pleased. You wear it a few times and get some spots on it. Seems a shame to send it back then, and anyhow, many of those who bought it said they could not equal it at twice the price. Of course, you have not had the time or energy to go in and compare prices yourself. Oh, well, it's a pretty good bargain, and too darned much trouble to send back now whether it is or not. Box it came in is probably thrown away. And so another sale is made. Not just the best kind of sale, of course, but probably the average sale.

Certain it is that the same principle holds true of almost any kind of selling. A friend of ours, for instance, sells yachts, some of them priced at over a million dollars. Do you suppose he goes or writes to J. P. Morgan and says:

"See here, J. P., that old yacht of yours is getting a little down at heel. The mud guards are scratched and the upholstery is getting moth-eaten, and as for the engine—it's so wheezy that when you start from the float, every old tub around ups anchor and poles away, for fear you will bust and spread yourself over the landscape before you reach Hoboken. Honest, J. P., the original Model T Ford couldn't rattle worse than that contraption you call a yacht. Better let me enter your order for a real boat, old scout. Now how about it?"

This man has been instrumental in selling more than $25,000,000 worth of yachts, but I do not think any of them were sold in just that way. No, indeed.

When a man gets on his prospect list, nothing crude like that ever happens to him. He gets some interesting little circulars showing pictures of the latest in yachts, with just an adroit suggestion of how fine it would be to forget the office for a few weeks or months, forget the work-a-day world, and go cruising through the Caribbean, or around the South Sea Islands, or wherever life and adventure beckon.

Then after a few of these, the first time a new and especially attractive boat is ready for its trial cruise, Mr. Prospect receives a special delivery letter or telegram somewhat along these lines:

> *"New Asterbilt yacht ready for trial spin next Thursday, the 10th. Mr. Asterbilt is making up special party for a few pleasant hours on Sound and begs that you and Mrs. Prospect will honor him. Boat leaves Yacht Club dock at ten sharp. R. S. V. R"*

Does Mr. Prospect answer? And especially Mrs. Prospect! I give you three guesses. And when they are safely aboard, along with a number of other "big business men and their wives—mostly prospects like themselves—are things made comfortable for them? I'll say they are! It is perfect luxury afloat.

Nothing so gross as a salesman ever approaches them on a trip like that. True, they are shown over the boat by officials of the company. And every point of interest is called to their attention, even as with the automobile salesman. They go through the salon, the cabins, even down to the engine room so spick-and-span it would not seem out of place as an adjunct to a drawing room. They take the wheel a while, get the feel of the boat, begin thinking of all the things they could do if they had one like it.

And just about then, along comes one of these officials with a picture of the new boat they are building for Mr. Van Spiffiingen—a very wonderful boat, but some people prefer a bit more speed, or more beam, or whatnot, and Mr. Prospect has a chance to air his preference. And isn't that peculiar, but they have a boat in the building with those very features. Here are the plans. And before he knows it, Mr. Prospect has signed on the dotted line and is now Mr. Customer, soon to take a party out on a trial spin on his boat.

Wherein is the difference? The yacht sale runs into bigger figures and employs a bit more finesse—that's all. In its essence, it is the circus barker and his helpers all over again. And though the method may vary, the psychology back of it is necessary in every sale that is made.

Particularly is this true of selling by mail. Why should you buy a coat from John Blair, whom you have never seen, when there is a perfectly good store a couple of blocks away, where you can look over the stock of coats, try on as many as you like, and if you fail to find one that fits you exactly, you can have one altered until it does. Why should you take the trouble and risk of sending for a coat by mail when it is so much easier to get one at home?

For two reasons only: first, because you are convinced that you save money by so doing. Second, and just as important, because John Blair makes it even easier for you to get his coat than to go to the neighborhood store. And the same principles apply to every sale made by mail. Just listen to these few typical examples of successful ways of "supplying that impulse."

DON'T DECIDE ABOUT buying now. You can do that later. Simply return the special FREE TRIAL Card, and by return mail will come the Blank machine, all charges prepaid. Then, after 6 days' examination—after you have had plenty of chance to try it and prove it—if it is not all we say and more, send it back at our expense. We'll pay the charges both ways. Could we give you any stronger evidence of our faith in the Blank machine?

Let me just prove what it will mean to you. This will not entail the slightest obligation on your part. Fill out the card and mail it—that's all. We'll do the rest.

Figure it out for yourself—harness, feed, labor, veterinary bills—all the items your horse and wagon delivery cost you. Quite a sum, eh!

Now if you'll pick up that pencil you were figuring with a moment ago, and fill out the attached card, we'll tell you all about Ford motor trucks—how they are increasing efficiency and decreasing costs for people in your line of business, folks you know personally.

Just send the enclosed card today. It doesn't obligate you in the least. We are only too glad to thoroughly demonstrate. No harm done if you don't keep it.

Just fill out the enclosed slip and mail it, and the samples will be on the way in time to start this department with next Saturday's sale. Remember, you risk nothing all you have to think about is your profit.

This puts you under not the slightest obligation. It simply gives us the chance to submit figures that you can check against the prices you have been paying— we're always glad to do that anyway, whether we get the particular job we figure on or not.

After a thorough examination and 10 days' trial, if you are convinced that you want an Excelle, you need send us only $5 then, and the balance in conveniently arranged payments over the next nine months. But if you don't want to keep the Excelle, remember you can return it without question, for you are under no obligation in accepting this free trial offer in this way.

This won't put you under the least obligation. If we can't show you that it is to your interest to take up this matter, it is our fault not yours. Just mail the card and let us put the facts before you. You must wear the smile of satisfaction, or it's no sale. That's our guarantee on every machine. Can you ask more! On that understanding, will you mail the enclosed blank?

Take us at our word—put us to the test—give us an opportunity to prove our claims to you. Use the postcard enclosed. Fill it out and send it to us.

A modern and actual Aladdin's lamp lies in the return card attached. Rub it with your pencil and your wish for full and complete particulars without obligation will come true.

———

Remember, an order is simply an opportunity for the Blank to sell itself to you.

There is no sale—no obligation to keep it—until you have used it in your own home for 30 days and are satisfied. Just let it show you what it can do.

———

John J. Jones, Chairman of the Board of the great Associated National Banks, was once asked how he managed to handle such an enormous volume of daily work demanding important executive decisions. "I never need to give more than one hour to the consideration of any question, however important," he answered, "because first, I get all the facts before me, and the time to decide is while the facts are fresh in mind."

———

Because you are likely to agree with Mr. Jones' sound conclusion, we are sending for your convenience a form on which to register your decision upon the important facts which this letter has placed before you. And there is a stamped, addressed envelope enclosed to bring it back to us, so that you may receive your first benefits from your decision without a minute's unnecessary delay.

———

Signing and sending the enclosed card puts the burden of proof upon us, and incurs no obligation.

I'm willing to do my part. Are you willing to put me to the test? Just fill in on the enclosed card the size tire your car takes—and watch results!

So don't file this away to think over. There's nothing to puzzle about, because you don't have to send one penny or promise anything, other than that if you don't like the Blank you will return it at the end of the week. That's easy, isn't it!

To prove it, all you have to do is fill in, sign and mail the card. After 30 days, you can return the Blank if you want to.

Try it out. Never mind what we say about the uses your clerks will get out of *it—find out!* It is easy. Just rather continue to use other send the card.

Use this machine at our expense for ten days. If you like it, keep it. If not, send it back to us, freight collect. This trial won't obligate you in any way, nor will it cost you a penny.

Will you check, on the enclosed card, the particular types of merchandise which would interest you most? In doing this, you will both acknowledge receipt of our catalog, and also enable us to keep you on the list for certain data of interest.

And remember, the book is free. To each of the first thousand manufacturers subscribing to the Blank Magazine, we will send a cloth-bound copy of this did 300-page book without charge. And even the magazine is no expense, for the $2 you pay for it will come back to you many times over before you have read half of the 12 issues.

We enclose letter the Railway Company wrote us. Please return it in the enclosed stamped, addressed envelope, and tell us what you think of our plan.

Tucked away in the inside pages of this letter, you will find a convenient postcard. Your name and address on that card will bring samples of Morco Flavors. These powerful, concentrated flavors possess three times the strength of ordinary extracts. You require only one-third the usual quantity. That's where the big saving comes in.

Take it home. Use the Quick-Lite 10 days. If you don't think it the most wonderful light you ever saw—if it isn't everything we claim it to be, just take it back to the dealer and he will refund your money. We give you this "10-day Visit" offer as an absolute guarantee of complete satisfaction. There are no strings to it. Buy a lamp. Use it 10 nights. If you don't want to keep it—if you would rather continue to use other means of lighting—take the Quick-Lite back to your dealer and get your money.

That's all you have to do—put your name on the enclosed card now, while this free 10-volume book offer is still open. We guarantee your satisfaction and delight. For if after receipt of books you are not more than pleased, send them back at our expense, and any money you may have paid will be returned at once.

YOUR READER, IN SHORT, is interested, but hasn't quite made up his mind. He balks at putting his name on the dotted line. "Some other time" "Tomorrow!" That little word "Tomorrow—Mahana"—is said to have been the cause of the Spanish people's decline. Certainly it has cost many a salesman and sales letter- writer his job, for more than all other causes put together, it has lost sales.

So do not give your prospect the chance to spring any "Mahana" upon you.

Beat him to it. Tell him not to decide now—on your main proposition. Instead, put his mind to working on some minor point—and you will find that a favorable decision on it will, in three cases out of four, carry the major proposition along with it!

Chapter 8 -
HOW TO PUT A HOOK INTO YOUR LETTERS

AS THE TAIL IS TO THE kite, as the rudder is to the ship, so is the close to any important letter. It may be a perfectly good letter aside from that. It may fit right in with the reader's thoughts, it may win his interest, it may spur him to action, but if it does not tell him *what* to do, if it does not provide a penalty for his not doing it, your prospect will slip away from you like a fish off the hook.

There is just one reason why anyone ever reads a letter you send him. He expects a reward. That is the key to holding his interest. All through your letter you keep leading him on, constantly feeding his interest, but always holding back something for the climax.

You come to it. You make your special offer. Your reader is impressed. He promises himself he will give it favorable consideration.

But you do not want favorable consideration. You want an order or a payment.

How are you going to get it? Start your impulse, as outlined in the last chapter.

Good! But if that does not work, what then? *Provide a penalty!*

There are only two reasons why your reader will do as you tell him to in your letter. The first is that you have made him want something so badly that of his own inertia he reaches out for your order card to get it. The other is that you have aroused in him the fear that he will lose something worthwhile if he does not do as you say.

It may be a delinquent debtor in fear of loss of credit standing or of court action. It may be a buyer fearing to lose his chance at a bargain. It may be the merchant fearing to lose your trade. It may be the ambitious youngster fearing to lose an opportunity for advancement. But unless your close can arouse in your reader the fear that he will lose something worthwhile if he does not do as you tell him, you will get no results.

So when you want to inspire fear, *be definite!* Be specific! If you are threatening suit, tell your reader that unless you have his remittance or a satisfactory explanation by a certain date, the account goes to your lawyer. If you are going to advance your price, and want to corral all the orders possible at the old figure, set a definite date for your advance. Or if you have only a few articles left, give the exact quantity.

It carries conviction, as you can see from these two examples—

> *On the 1st of October, the rate of the Messenger will go up to $1 a line. If you place your order before the 30th, you can buy space to be used any time before January 1st at 750 a line. After the 30th, positively no orders will be accepted at less than $1 a line. As a matter of fact, our circulation entitles us to $1 a line right now.*
>
> *Don't let this letter be covered up on your desk. Send the enclosed reservation right now, or instruct your advertising agent to reserve the space for you, and make sure of this big bargain.*

> *Only 46 sets left! The success of our special offer surpassed all expectations. It will be necessary to issue another edition at once. The style of binding will be changed, but otherwise the two editions will be the same. As we don't want to carry two*

styles on hand, we are willing to let you have one of the remaining 46 sets at the old price, although the increased cost of paper, printing and binding has forced us to raise the price of the new sets more than 50%.

MAKE YOUR READER FEEL that this is his last chance—keep your penalty dangling before his mind's eye, the money-saving lost, the opportunity missed. Put into your close the fear of consequences.

Finally, tell him what to do. Don't leave it to him to decide. We are all mentally lazy, you know, so dictate his action for him—get your suggester to working on him. If he is to do certain things, describe them. Tell him to put his name on the enclosed card, stamp and mail, or pin his check or dollar bill to this letter and return in the enclosed envelope. Here is the way others have done it successfully:

"NOW, WHAT AM I TO DO?" you ask. Simply send your order to me personally.

Just say—" Make my suit as you agreed in your letter." If you wish other samples or further information, we shall be more than glad to furnish them. But send your order first. Remember, we have material on hand sufficient for only 95 suits. While they last, you can get a made-to-measure, tailored-to-fit suit of our regular $75 quality, for only $37.50. But to do so, you have to be prompt.

Don't send me any money after the 1st. If you do, it will surely be returned, unless you are willing to pay me the new price of $50 a share instead of $40.

I have some regard for the men who made inquiries when our project was young before it fairly got under way. That is why I am including you in this offer because you were one of our original inquirers. Remember, no acceptance of your old price after the 1st. The stock is even now worth $50.

Such wonderful opportunities will of course be snapped up quickly. Our doors will open at 9 o'clock Monday morning, and to have the widest range of selection, you should not put off your visit a moment later than absolutely necessary.

It was necessary to place this large order to secure the sets at the lowest possible figure. Knowing that the number would exceed our weekly sales, we decided to offer these extra sets to some of the ambitious young men who have been writing us.

If you will fill out the enclosed scholarship blank and mail it right away, we will send you one of these handsome sets FREE, express prepaid. But this offer must be accepted before the 30th of this month. At the rate Scholarship Blanks are now coming in, it is more than likely that the available sets will all be gone by the 30th. It is necessary therefore that you send your application at once.

The demand has been large and there are only a few copies left but one of them will be yours when you have O.K.'d and mailed the enclosed card.

But you must act now. There are only 2700 copies of this book still on hand and no more can be printed at less than double the price. So pin your money to this letter and mail it today.

Remember, he who hesitates nowadays never gets a flash at fortune. The men who made millions in Texas oil lands are the men who dared, who went ahead unafraid, who plunged in on their own judgment—and didn't wait.

The saying that everything comes to him who waits may have been true a hundred years ago, when people had plenty of time to wait for the good things of life. But today the only one that things come to is the man who goes after them. The enclosed blank is your reservation for some of the good things of life. Will you mail it now—TODAY?

IT HAS BEEN PROVED that seven times out of ten your average business man will read the opening paragraph of an ordinary letter that is palpably not from a customer, take a cursory glance at the middle, and then jump to the last paragraph to see what it is all about, and how much it costs. So it is essential that you put a hook into that last paragraph.

Remember, too, that a successful close has two parts. The first is the persuasion and inducement. It shows your reader the gain that is his by ordering, the chances of loss he takes by delay. It emphasizes the guarantee and minimizes the cost.

When your reader gets that far, he is almost ready to act, but your close lacks a hook. What must he do to get all these things? *Tell him!* Make it so plain and easy he will not have a reason for not ordering. If you do not, you have not finished your letter, and lacking the barb of that hook, your reader is likely to lapse from his "almost ready" attitude back into indifference.

Chapter 9 -
THE SIX ESSENTIALS

TO SUM IT UP, EVERY good letter contains these six essential elements:

1. *The opening,* which gets the reader's attention by fitting in with his train of thought and establishes a point of contact with his interests, thus exciting his curiosity and prompting him to read further.

2. *The description or explanation,* which pictures your proposition to the reader by first outlining its important features, then filling in the necessary details.

3. *The motive or reason why,* which creates a longing in the reader's mind for what you are selling, or impels him to do as you want him to, by describing— not your proposition but what it will do for him—the comfort, the pleasure, the profit he will derive from it.

4. *The proof or guarantee,* which offers to the reader proof of the truth of your statements, or establishes confidence by a money-back-if-not-satisfied guarantee.

5. *The snapper or penalty,* which gets immediate action by holding over your reader's head the loss in money or prestige or opportunity that will be his if he does not act at once.

6. *The close,* which tells the reader just what to do and how to do it, and makes it easy for him to act at once.

These rules, of course, are for the man or woman who is studying the art of writing resultful letters. After a time, they come to be a sort of second nature, so that you weigh each of these features without being conscious that you are doing so. You may even mix them all up into one grand goulash, so that to the beginner they will seem to be not there at all, but they or their close relatives are in every successful letter.

Rules, however, are merely the start. They are the mechanics of a letter. Real letter-writing only starts there. It is getting the feel of your message that counts.

I remember the first sales letter I ever wrote. I knew as little about the writing of letters as any one who ever took his typewriter in hand to tackle the job. But I was full of an idea, and it came out all over that letter. And that is what counts.

I was doing mining engineering at the time, in a little town called Powellton, in West Virginia. We had an unusually good vein of gas coal, which was called the Powellton Seam; and the 200 old style, beehive ovens, with which we turned out Powellton Coke.

Like all the other mines in the district, we depended for business upon brokers in the big towns. They would contract with the large users for so many carloads of coal or coke, of a certain general grade, and then place their orders with whichever mines made them the lowest price, allowing them the greatest margin. The result was that all the mines were in much the same boat, whether their coal happened to be better or worse. When times were good they bid against each other for laborers, and between the lack of them and the lack of cars they were able to run the mines only three or four days a week. When times were bad they underbid each other for the little business available, and managed to work only one or two days a week.

That condition had been general for a good many years, with our mines as with practically all the others in the district. And there was no reason to think it would not continue indefinitely, as, in fact, it has with many of the mines in that district.

But from much cogitation, there one day dawned upon us an idea so obvious you will wonder why we did not think of it first thing. It was this: We had an unusually good grade of gas coal and a splendid coke.

There must be certain purposes for which that coal and that coke would produce far better results than any other made. If we could find these purposes, the businesses that needed coal and coke for them would cheerfully pay any reasonable premium for our particular product, and not only would we make more money, but we would cease to be dependent upon the whims of the brokers and would be sure of a regular volume of orders through good times and bad.

So we started experimenting, and found that for gas-making purposes we had easily the best coal in the district. Figured on the basis of cubic feet of gas produced, to say nothing of the by-products, any gas company could well afford to pay from 25 to 33 percent more for our coal.

That was all we needed. From that moment, every gas company within a radius of several hundred miles was our target. We disregarded the usual "per ton" prices to a great extent, centering our whole argument upon how many cubic feet of gas they got from each pound of coal, and what that gas cost them, including the delivered price of their coal.

> *How much are you paying per cubic foot for your gas? [was the basis of our letters]. If we can show you how to cut the cost by a fourth, are you interested enough to prove it? The Blank Gas Company of Cincinnati has cut its costs by more than that, and here are the figures as given in a letter from their Superintendent. [Here we quoted exact figures and costs]. The Bank Company of Indianapolis and [here we mentioned*

four or five other companies well and favorably known to the trade] have had similar experiences. We'll be glad to send you the exact figures from each if you will take the time to read them.

But better than any figures from other plants is this chance to write new figures of your own in your plant. Send the enclosed card, without money. On receipt of it, we will ship you a carload of Powellton screened gas coal, our regular standard quality.

Test it. Try it any way you wish. At the end of your tests, figure how much gas you get per pound of coal, and what that gas cost you! If you don't find that the Powellton Coal has saved you at least 25% on your cost, then that carload we send you won't cost you one cent. But if you do see where you can save from 25 to 33% of the cost of your gas, then you are to give us your contract for all the gas coal you use for the next year, at a price of $1.25 per ton f.o.b. Powellton, W.Va. Remember, no saving—no cost. But if we save you 25%, we get your contract. Is it a go?

I knew none of the rules of letter-writing. I could not have told you the difference between a clincher and a monkey wrench. But was bubbling over with enthusiasm for our idea, and that enthusiasm must have permeated our letters, for we got so many orders from gas companies, it kept us pumping to fill them all. And what was more to the point, they stuck. When I left Powellton, we still had on our books nearly every gas company we had ever put there.

One would stray away now and then, of course, lured by the sire song of a bargain. When that happened, we said nothing—just got a few average samples of the other man's coal and sent them, with samples of ours, to a laboratory for comparative test. When the reports came back, we carried them out in figures of the cost of the coal and the final cost of the gas per cubic foot and sent the result without comment to the superintendent or other responsible executive of the gas company. In most cases the business was soon on our books again.

The coal problem solved, we set about finding a similar solution of the coke question, for the gas companies preferred screened coal, which meant that all the dust coal or slack was left us for cooking purposes.

We had made frequent analysis of our coke, of course, and knew that it was unusually low in sulfur, phosphorus and ash. So we set out to see which type of foundryman considered these qualities most valuable.

We soon learned that to the maker of steel rails, phosphorus was anathema, so we had little difficulty in persuading the Ashland Steel Company that a coke as low in Phosphorus as ours was easily worth 25 cts. more a ton than any other they could buy. 25 cts. a ton doesn't sound like much, but when you multiply it by sixty to ninety tons a day, which was what the Ashland Steel required, it soon runs into money.

That was a good start so, much encouraged, we looked around for others. And in the makers of stoves and ranges we found possible customers who were quite as particular about sulfur as the Steel Company had been about phosphorus. In thin castings like those needed in stoves and ranges, sulfur means bubbles and cracks, and costs more money than any saving in price can possibly make up for.

But stove founders were, for the most part, located pretty far away from us, and other good cokes just about as low as ours in sulfur content were as readily available to them. To get their business on other than a price basis, we had to find some better argument than low sulfur content.

We worked on that for quite some time, talked to different founders to get a line on their problems, studied numerous books on the subject and finally stumbled on the answer almost by accident.

It happened that we had been figuring on a big contract with the Bucks Stove and Range Company of St. Louis. They were one of the most efficiently run concerns in the business, and they wanted the best, regardless of what it cost.

So before placing their contract, they bought a carload of coke from each of half a dozen concerns whose analysis and claims seemed to indicate that they were in the running.

We had shipped them a carload and intended to run out to St. Louis in order to be on the spot when the contract was awarded, so that if it seemed that a last-minute reduction of 10 or 15 cts. a ton would turn the scales in our favor, we could throw it in. When lo and behold, without notice of any kind, in came the contract by mail at the price we had originally quoted! To say that we were pleasantly surprised was putting it mildly. But we didn't let either our pleasure or our surprise get in the way of the fact that here was probably the answer to our problem. If our coke stood out so well in a comparative test that we had landed the Bucks order without effort, in the face of the best cokes and the best salesmen that the Connellsville could show, then there must be something unusual about our coke that every other stove founder ought to know. And we lost no time in setting out for St. Louis to learn what it was.

And here is what we found: Its high carbon content and low ash gave Powellton Coke a heating power that would melt an unusual amount of iron and a structure that supported a phenomenal weight, with the result that where a good coke did well to melt eight or nine tons of iron to one of coke, ours melted as high as fifteen tons of iron to one of coke! Figuring the price of the coke at $7 a ton delivered, it cost the Bucks Stove and Range Company 80 to 90 cts. to melt a ton of iron with ordinary coke, whereas with Powellton Coke it cost them only

47 cts.! Can you wonder that they gave us the order without urging or bargaining?

Our problem was solved, and, as is often the case, through no skill of ours. The Lord had been good to us in the kind of coal he gave us, and instead of patting ourselves on the back, we should have been kicked for not cashing in sooner on our products' peculiar advantages.

But we were too happy over having found the answer to do any worrying about what was past and done with. It took us just about three days to get a letter into the mails to every stove founder within five hundred miles of us. This, you must remember, was back in 1907 or 1908, when Bryan was still a name to attract attention anywhere.

———

WHEN BILL BRYAN FIRST sprung his 16 to 1 ratio upon a waiting world, founders and business men generally called it visionary and impractical—said it wouldn't work.

So when Bill Smith, Cupola Foreman for the Bucks Stove & Range Company of St. Louis, proudly strode into the President's office with his report of a 15 to I melt, he wasn't surprised to meet with only skepticism on the part of that official.

"You're getting your politics mixed with your melting figures!" accused the Boss. Bill may lack some of the eloquence of his namesake, but no one ever accused him of running away from a scrap. So the upshot of it was that the President agreed to be on hand at the next melt.

Sure enough, Bill's figures proved to be right! They didn't equal Bryan's 16 to 1, but they averaged a good 15 tons of iron to every one of coke!

Of course, Bill modestly disclaims the credit. "Any one could do it with that coke," he says. "It's got a structure that'd carry the Eiffel tower. And as for sulfur bubbles—it just never heard of such words."

And that's the reason Powellton Coke gets the Bucks Stove & Range contract this year, in direct competition with and after thorough tests of every good coke on the market. That's the reason the Gallipolis Stove Company, the Huntington Range Company and a dozen others have been using Powellton Coke for years.

Of course, some of them stray away occasionally. We're none of us proof against the siren song of low price, but when they begin to figure the cost of their coke in tons of iron melted, as the Bucks Stove & Range Company did; when they find that on this basis Powellton Coke is costing them only 470 a ton of melted iron against 800 to 900 for any other brand, and when they add to that the cost of scrap castings due to sulfur and phosphorus, they always come back, and it's a long time before they stray again.

If you figure your coke cost, not on the delivered price of the coke, but on tons of iron melted—if you are buying high carbon heat-content, and not sulfur, ash and phosphorus—we have some figures that will interest you.

May we send them?

THAT LETTER BROUGHT home the bacon. For a while we had almost a monopoly of the stove and range business in our territory. We did not keep it altogether, because good coke structure depends largely upon skill in making the coke, and other ovens with the right kind of coal succeeded in making almost as good a coke as ours. With intensive study, they found ways of loading the furnace so that their coke would melt just about as high a percentage of iron as ours.

But do not imagine we were resting on our laurels, or out playing golf all this time. We realized it would not be long until some one caught up to where we were then, so we tried to keep at least one good jump ahead.

We tested not only our coal and coke, but different ways of screening the one and making the other. We tried cooking longer and shorter periods, charging the ovens with bigger or smaller charges—everything, in fact, that we could think of that might make our product better.

And we did not stop with our own product. We had numbers of experiments made in the more effective use of our coal and coke We had never heard of the rule that a letter should talk—not about your own product but about the pleasure or profit your customer will get out of it, but we had learned from long experience that coal and coke were drugs on the market and could only be sold on a price basis, whereas cubic feet of gas, or thermal units of steam, or melted tons of iron were things that sold themselves.

In line with our idea of making every possible improvement in. our product, we got a few books on letter-writing and applied the principles outlined in them to our letters. I remember the first set of books we got. It was System's "Business Correspondence Library[1]"—three volumes—and it became our Bible for direct-mail work Looking back on it now, I do not believe we could have found a better ground-work for our studies. Certain it is that it helped us to sell many thousands of tons of coal and coke, when without it we might have lost the sales. I think it is out of print now, but next to Herbert Watson's "Applied Business Correspondence," I believe it had helped more men to a knowledge of how to use letters for profit that any set of books ever written.

---

1. https://archive.org/details/cu31924013879253

John Blair, founder of the New Process Company of Warten, Pa. once told me the same thing. His introduction to good letter-writing came from the same little set of three books—after he had made him bow with a few successful efforts of his own, about which more anon.

To go back to our interrupted labors: Starting in 1907 or 1908, and continuing for five years, we sold practically all the products of our mines and ovens by mail. We used dozens of different letters and circulars, with all kinds of variants upon the one appeal, but unfortunately my book of letters was lost a few years ago, and the company had then changed hands, so the only sample I have to show is the letter quoted above.

It was about this time I had the good fortune to meet Thomas H. Beck, then sales manager—now president of Collier's. He had been sales manager of Proctor & Gamble, the Ivory Soap people, where he was responsible for as revolutionary an idea in its way as was ours of selling cubic feet of gas and tons of melt.

Soap flakes, it seems, were sold to laundries by the barrel of so many pounds weight. One barrel of soap was considered much like another, so sales were made almost entirely on price. Then it occurred to Tom Beck to have Ivory Soap flakes analyzed and the results compared with analysis made in their laboratory of all the competing brands. What was his surprise and delight to find that the competing brands contained something like (let us say) 15 percent water, to only about 5 percent water for Ivory!

If a barrel of soap cost $2, a laundryman could pay Ivory $2.20 and be getting his actual soap content for the same price per pound that he was paying the $2 competitor. If in addition he was paying $1 a barrel for freight or delivery service, that made an extra premium of 10 cts. he was handing to Ivory's competitor.

It did not take Tom Beck more than half a minute to figure out the possibilities that this opened up. As soon as they could be got into the mail, he had letters on the way to every laundry in his territory asking them whether they were buying soap or water, suggesting that it might be cheaper to get their own water from the faucet rather than have it freighted all the way from the factory to them, and then be charged for it at soap prices in addition.

To say that he started a furor among soap makers is putting it mildly.

The net result to him was that it enabled him to land the far bigger job with Collier's, and to me that it gave me a sympathetic ear into which to pour an idea I had long been nursing for selling Collier books by mail.

Chapter 10 -
THE IDEAL SALES LETTER

YOU REMEMBER THE NEWSPAPER editor's description of the ideal wedding: "Fake a beautiful heiress " he said, "have her elope with the chauffeur. Let the irate father pursue with a shot-gun and a high-powered car. Throw in a smash-up, a heroic rescue and a nip-and-tuck finish—and you have the ideal situation dear to tabloid readers."

And his advice to cub reporters was to go to every wedding with that ideal situation in mind, see how many of the dramatic elements from that situation could be found in the function he was attending and build his story around them.

Much the same thought can be used in writing letters. No matter what the product or service you are writing about, first put yourself in the place of your prospective customer. Think of every property you could possibly desire in such a product or service. Think of everything you would like to have it do for you. Work out the ultimate ideal, then write a letter that stresses every desirable point of that ideal product.

Here, for instance, is the basis for an ideal bargain appeal on linen tablecloths.

Read it, then turn back to the old "damaged-set" letter and see how closely we came to the ideal in our offerings with it:

WE ARE MANUFACTURERS of Linen Tablecloths. We import the finest linen direct from Belfast-linen with the sheen of satin—so heavy it will stand alone, so strong it will wear forever.

Linen like that is worth a king's ransom, and costs just about that in the best stores. But by selling it to you direct, with no wholesaler or middleman or high store expenses or service charges, we can save you half the usual price.

But that isn't all! Even at half the regular retail price, this linen is so costly that you may feel you still cannot afford it. But in manufacturing thousands of these fine tablecloths, we turn out an occasional one with some slight flaw in it—perhaps an uneven hem, perhaps a slight discoloration in some tiny spot—not enough to be apparent to the eye of any but the expert, but still not up to our standard of perfection.

Over the past few months, we have accumulated perhaps thirty or forty of these technically imperfect tablecloths. While they last, you can have one for one- third off our already low price!

Remember, though, we have only 30 or 40 of these, and we may not have another for months, so if you want to even see one, it behooves you to use the enclosed order form quickly.

WHEN YOU HAVE YOUR ideal letter written to your satisfaction, let it cool for a day. The next day, go over it and cross out every descriptive phrase and adjective that cannot honestly be applied to your product. You will be surprised at how many you have left—more than enough to write the finest sort of a letter that will build a picture in your reader's mind so desirable that he will scarcely be able to refrain from ordering.

There is an old saying, you know, that there is nothing you can say about a 50 cent cigar that you cannot say about a 5 cent one—and the Cremo advertising seems to be proving the truth of it. You see, the only difference between an expensive product and one of ordinary price is usually one of degree. In a general way, they look alle, they are made of much the same type of material, they will do the same things. The difference is in the degree of pleasure or satisfaction they will bring. And this is largely in the mind of the buyer.

So your job is to build a picture in his mind's eye of what he will get from your product or service. Build it with bricks he can handle, i.e., with words and mental images that are familiar to him. Do not exaggerate—or he will refuse to believe in it and kick the whole structure over disgustedly, like a child trying to build with blocks a house that will not come out right. But keep it attractive. Keep it desirable—more desirable far than the money or the time or the trouble it takes to build it.

Do not make the mistake of tying to stress in your letter all the points of your product. You can list them in a separate folder and make your letter the stronger for it. But find the one point on which your sale is likely to hang and build your letter around it. Let that be the focal point of your mental image, your picture, and let every word in it be a brush stroke that adds clearness and power to that one focal point.

Then remember that it is not enough merely to tell your reader to order now, or "Mail the enclosed card at once!" Why must he do this? What will he gain by doing it now? What will he lose by delay?

You must dangle certain bait before his eyes. You must hold over his head a "Sword of Damocles," the thread of which may be cut at any moment. Set a time beyond which orders will not be accepted. Or give a valid reason why the supply is strictly limited. Or announce an increase in price that takes effect on a certain date. Or make a special combination offer, good only for a limited time.

But whatever you do, make it sound as though you mean it. If you set a time limit, say positively that no orders will be accepted beyond that date. If you announce a raise in price, tell them there will be no last-minute concessions. All orders not mailed by a certain date will take the higher price. Be definite— and be positive! You will lose a few last-minute orders, but you will gain ten times the number in those who are impelled to act the moment they read the letter—while the order card is in their hands—for fear if they lay it down they will delay and be too late.

These are the important factors of a successful letter. There are others, however, that add to or take away from their effectiveness.

The first essential is to get your reader to look inside the envelope. That may sound simple—and is simple on ordinary correspondence—but when you have been circularizing in a large way and people recognize your envelopes as circulars at sight, then it becomes a problem.

Some people depend upon "teasers" on the outside of the envelope to arouse the reader's curiosity and make him took at the letter to see what it is all about.

A really effective "teaser" is good, but the effective ones are scarce. As a general rule, it is better to try to make your envelope so personal looking and so attractive that the reader will at least want to know whom it is from and what it is about.

This can be done in various ways. If your name is too well known and your mere comer card brands the envelope as containing a circular, it frequently pays to use a box number in the comer, with an armorial design or a monogram or some such attractive insignia under it.

Using a window envelope sometimes helps, as does a change in the color of the envelope or in the size. If your mailings have been going in a No. 6 envelope, change to a baronial at times, from that to a Monarch, then to a No. 9 and back to your No. 6, varying your comer card on all, and sometimes changing the color as well as the size of your envelope.

One concern makes a specialty of letters on pseudo-telegraph forms, mailed in envelopes that look almost exactly like the yellow window envelopes the Western Union uses for telegrams. We have tried them and found them very effective as a variation from our usual forms.

Another makes a "giant" telegram of it, using 18-point type, a giant envelope and a pseudo-telegraph form inside to fit it. This in our experience has been even more effective than the other. But again it is just a novelty and will wear out quickly if used too much.

Such novelties, however, are invaluable to the man who does much circularizing, for they keep his appeal from going stale. People never throw away his letters unopened because they are never able to discount in advance what is inside them. But when they have taken your reader into your letter, their job is done. From there on, it is up to you to win his interest and turn it into a sale.

What is the most important factor in the making of your sale? Your letter! The circular helps, and the order card makes it easier—but the letter must carry the load. If you have not the stuff in it, it does not matter where else you have it. It will not do you much good.

So put your best efforts into your letter. Keep an "idea file" of good starters, good descriptions, good closers, good pointers of all kinds—not to copy, but to inspire you to new and better ideas. There is nothing like glancing over a few such ideas to stimulate your own brain cells into action. And always remember that the point which sells your customer is not what your product is, *but what it will do for him!*

Remember, too, that the purpose of a letter is to put ideas into your reader's head, so be careful not to put in negative ones that you will have to take out again before you can make a sale.

Some people will tell you never to write long letters, others never to make them short. Both are wrong—as didactic extremists usually are. As a general proposition, it is advisable to make your letter short and snappy when you are trying for inquiries and all you want is to win enough of the prospect's interest to make him ask for further particulars.

Before a man will definitely commit himself to buy, however, he wants to know all about the thing you are offering, and you cannot tell him that in a short letter. So tell your story, no matter how long or how short it may be, striving simply to keep it interesting. The only safe measure you can apply is the one Lincoln gave when someone asked him how long a man's legs should be: "Long enough to reach the ground!"

Postscript

PEOPLE WILL GIVE, WHEN you have stirred their emotions. People will invest, when you have aroused their cupidity. And people want to know the future, so if you can persuade them that you are any sort of a Seer or a Prophet, they will buy your forecasting service.

It all comes back to the point we made in the beginning—"What do they want?" What is the bait that will attract your fish and make them bite? Find that—and you will be as successful in bringing back orders as any angler can be with a properly baited hook in bringing in the fish.

Addenda

THESE SALES LETTERS are reproduced here so that you can have a guide and examples of the many letters Collier talks about in these few chapters.

Addendum 1 – the Letter Book Sales Letter

THIS LETTER IS THOUGHT to have been written by Robert Collier himself, even though it didn't have his name signed to it.

The Robert Collier Letter Book

The Greatest of All Direct Mail Books

Dear Sir:

When a man can turn an $80,000 loss as of June 1st into a $121,000 Net Profit as of December 31st, entirely with letters -

When he can sell, by mail $3,000,000 worth of traveling bags – take 400,000 pairs or returned silk stockings at the regular dealer's price and dispose of them by mail, at a profit -

When he can increase gross sales in three years time from $2,000,000 a year to $6,000,000 a year for one concern, and then go and do just as big a job for two other companies in completely different lines of business – all through the use of clever, well written letters -

Then there has to be something so fundamentally sound about his way of writing and using letters that it would pay you as a man interested in making more money to try the same methods in your business.

Of course, we are referring to the world famous Robert Collier techniques of selling by mail – now available -

THE ROBERT COLLIER LETTER BOOK

For more than 20 years, Robert Collier successfully sold anything and everything by mail. During that time, he was in charge of direct mail selling for Colliers, Review of Reviews, New Process Company, and many others. He sold considerably more than $20,000,000 worth of goods by mail, including $2,000,000 worth of O. Henry stories, over $3,000,000 worth of Well's Outline Of History and millions of dollars worth of all manner of products from coal and coke to ladies' dresses and men's socks.

In THE ROBERT COLLIER LETTER BOOK, you get every one of the hundreds of sound, tested plans that worked so profitably for Mr. Collier and many famous firms...countless specimens of actual letters and circulars, including a short, clear discussion by the author of what exactly made them work – what made them pull in orders. Here, for you, are money-making plans that you can put to work for greater returns in your direct mail campaign. Plans like these -

The direct mail strategy that sold one million copies of the Book of Etiquette after it had gathered dust for fifteen years in Doubleday's stock room.

The letter that actually sold 50,000 traveling bags, reviving the New Process Company at a time when it was in the red for $80,000.

The direct mail ideas that induced nearly half of the nation's top executives to subscribe to newly published Business Week magazine

These and hundreds of other sales boosting methods in THE ROBERT COLLIER LETTER BOOK are yours to be used by you, no matter what your objective may be.

Suppose you're in business for yourself, but don't have the money you'd like to spend on advertising. Chapter 22 shows you how one lady's ready-to-wear dress dealer achieved outstanding profits from a $50-a-week investment in direct mail. Or suppose you've always wanted to build up a bigger and better mailing list of your own – of proven buyers. Chapter 11 shows you step-by-step how such firms as William H. Wise and Company, and the New Process Company go about getting just such results.

Say you have a new product to introduce to the public, but can't afford to take a chance and gamble. Chapter 20 shows you how to safely forecast its selling possibilities – the same system Robert Collier used on one product to pull in one million dollars worth of orders during the first six months of business.

The same thing goes for any question or problem that comes up in your direct mail work. You can use this book and its techniques as a jumping-off place – find out for yourself what others have accomplished when faced with problems so similar to the ones you have. Regardless of what your sales objective is, simply turn to THE ROBERT COLLIER LETTER BOOK and find actual, tested profit plans that accomplished such a varied amount of objectives for Robert Collier and others.

Mr. W.F. Rehbock of the Foley Manufacturing Company, Minneapolis, after reading and using THE ROBERT COLLIER LETTER BOOK, in its previous edition wrote:

We made a test mailing of 3,000 letters along the lines suggested by Mr. Collier, and 3,000 of our regular letters which had been getting good results for several years, and we were amazed to find that we increased the pull 50%.

Why not see the book for yourself – Examine it and use it for 10 days at our risk!

Naturally, we think the book is absolutely tops – and we're pretty well qualified to judge its merits because of our own direct mail experience – therefore, we must recommend it to every advertising man, every manufacturer, every individual interested in making money selling by direct mail. But, it's only after you see and use this great book yourself that you can determine how valuable it can be to you.

Mail the enclosed card and get your copy on this 10 day free trial offer. Then, see for yourself what a help it can be whenever you're stuck for a new idea and fresh approach. When you're thoroughly convinced, send us your check for $10 plus a few cents to cover postage and shipping. However, if for some reason you're not entirely satisfied, return the book to us and you'll be under no further obligation. Fair enough?

Sincerely yours,

Addendum 2 – the 15 Million Dollar Sales Letters

THIS COLLECTION WAS found floating around the Internet, apparently written during Collier's lifetime. Please enjoy.

SELLING BY MAIL can be the easiest and least expensive method of selling your services or commodities.

It can also be the most difficult and the most expensive method of doing the job.

It all depends on the method you use in presenting your offering to your prospects; it depends on the kind of a letter you send to them.

To write such a letter, a message that explains concisely yet completely and in an action- compelling manner what you have to offer, is a job that demands the services of an expert versed in every one of the thousand phases of selling and one with many years of successful mail order experience at his command.

If you would choose the one man in the United States who could write for you a sales letter that would produce the results you desire, you would probably ask Robert Collier to do the job.

Backed by many years of success in the field of selling by mail, selling every commodity from trench machinery to fertilizers, books and raincoats, stocks and bonds and services, he has placed hundreds of millions of dollars into the pockets of the clients for whom he has written his master sales letter.

As a consequence, he is today, America's premier writer of successful selling letters. We asked Mr. Collier to select from the many thousands of sales letters considered the best of them all. It was a difficult job to pick fifteen of the best from a list of ten thousand of the best - but the job is finished and here are the letters.

These are the fifteen letters considered the best ever written by the man acknowledged to be the best writer of sales letters in America today. They have been actually tested, they have been actually used, and they actually sold over one million dollars of services and merchandise.

These letters will sell for you. Choose those that are applicable to your own business. Alter them only to such an extent as to accord with the products and services you have to sell. But it will pay you, too, to study them all, for they all contain the essential elements that enter into every successful sales letter.

home?trk=nav_responsive_tab_homeThey contain ideas that you may apply successfully in sales letters of your own dictation.

Letter 1 - The Lowly Penny Will Often Do The Trick

HERE IS A LETTER TO which a new penny was pasted. In conjunction with the figures given, the penny aroused an amazing amount of attention.

The idea could readily be used by Insurance Companies, Savings Banks and the like. It was also used with unusual results by an association trying to build a membership for the purpose of cutting the cost of government.

IT IS A MARVELOUS THING -

The Power of Money to Make More Money!

Just this little insignificant penny, saved each week since the start of the Loan and Saving Association, would today amount to $75.00 - and of that $75.00, $50.00 WOULD BE INTEREST DIVIDENDS.

$1.00 saved each week would today amount to $7,500.00! THAT IS THE WAY MONEY GROWS!

No matter what his beliefs, every man will agree that the Scriptures contain some of the oldest and greatest truths known to mankind. There is one truth that the Wise Men of old felt to be so important, that they repeated it no less than six times in the very first chapter of the Bible, and referred to it throughout both Old and New Testaments.

This age-old truth is that EVERYTHING INCREASES AFTER ITS KIND! Plant a seed of corn, and you reap ears of corn. Plant thistles, and you grow a profusion of thistles. Plant money, and your money comes back to you after many days, increased a hundred- fold!

What harvest do YOU want to reap ten or fifteen years from now? Money to put your children through college, or start them in a business of their own? Security for yourself? Financial Independence?

You have only to set your goal in order to win it. The price of $5,000.00 or of $50,000.00 is only so many seeds of savings. $5.00 saved each week at the Loan and Savings Association will in about 13 Years amount to $5,000.00 $25.00 each week will grow to $25,000.00.

And mind you, here is the part that counts. Of that $25,000.00 only $16,250.00 represents money paid in by you. The rest - $8,750.00 - is GROWTH INCREASE!

Do you know any other way you can buy $25,000 as surely, as safely - and pay so little for it? Do you know any way you can buy $25,000 or any other sum, and pay for it in little, convenient installments each week that never depreciates in value, which are like seeds sown in good ground that keep growing and growing, year after year, always ready to give you more than you sow.

How much do you want to buy - $1,000.00 - $5,000.00 - $25,000.00? How much do you want to give to your youngster when he goes to college, or gets married, or starts in business? Here is the one sure and easy way of having that money when you want it. $1.00 a week now, means $1,000.00 thirteen years from now.

$5.00 a week means $5,000.00.

What will you start with - $1.00 - $5.00 - $10.00? "To begin", says Ansonius, "it is to be half done".

Will you begin NOW - TODAY? Will you fill out the little form attached, pin your check, dollar bills or stamps to it covering your first remittance and mail it back in the enclosed envelope? Will you save the first $1.00 on your $1,000.00, or the first $25.00 on your $25,000.00 TODAY?

Sincerely, _______________

Letter 2 - How Handkerchiefs Were Sold By Mail

A FEW YEARS AGO, A merchant in the clothing business in Buffalo failed. While he was waiting for the bankruptcy proceedings to be closed, he had no money and little credit. But he did have a family, and he had to do something to keep them from starving.

So he got a friend to advance him a few dollars and with that he bought some cheap knitted ties, and started mailing them - without orders of any kind to lists of likely buyers. With the ties, he sent a letter, offering the ties at 50 cents apiece, and enclosing postage for their return or for remittance.

Within a few months he is said to have cleared $200,000. In five years, it is reported that he made a couple of million. Similar offers were speedily made by dozens of other concerns. Here is the letter that successfully sold some hundreds of thousands of initialled handkerchiefs by this unique method.

Here's the most unusual offer you've ever received.

For years, it's been the custom among well-dressed men who were fastidious about their handkerchiefs to have BOTH their initials embroidered on them. But up to now, they've always had to order them specially at considerable expense.

For there were so many combinations of initials (630 to be exact) that no store could possibly carry them all in stock.

The result has been that fine quality handkerchiefs individually monogrammed have cost from 75 cents to $1.00 each. (Your wife will quickly verify this.) Now, we've conceived the idea of monogramming handkerchiefs without orders (in quantities that would keep the cost low) and sending them by mail to a carefully selected list of Business Men who would appreciate the wonderful opportunity afforded them.

You are one of the men we selected. Your handkerchiefs are enclosed - four of them monogrammed especially for you WITH BOTH YOUR OWN INITIALS.

These handkerchiefs are of fine quality, are fully-sized - 18 inches square and have a neatly hemstitched border. You will readily see that such handkerchiefs should cost 75 cents each when specially embroidered in silk with your initials.

If you'd like to keep these handkerchiefs, send us - not 75 cents each, not over 50 cents each - ONLY $1 FOR THE WHOLE FOUR. You can easily do it by slipping your check or money order in the enclosed envelope.

But, if you don't want to keep the handkerchiefs, just put them back in the envelope, paste the enclosed label and stamp over the address and shoot them back to us.

Isn't that a fair way to do business? It's the only way we know in which individually initialled handkerchiefs can be sold so reasonably.

When you send us the $1, in full payment for the handkerchiefs, please do not return the label with the stamp attached. Thank you! Every penny counts in selling handkerchiefs in this unusual way.

Yours for unusual handkerchief value, P.S. There's a birthday or anniversary coming up soon for some man you know, and you'll be looking for just such an attractive gift as those individually monogrammed handkerchiefs. Why no double the amount of your remittance now, tell us his initials, and we'll get the handkerchiefs off at once - either to him or to you!

Letter 3 - Can High Priced Articles Be Sold By Mail?

YES... THOUGH IT IS necessary to first use the inquiry-bringing type of letter to winnow out the few interested people, and then keep after those few with a whole series of letters until you land their orders.

$25,000,000 worth of yachts were sold by mail this way. Inquiry-bringing letters and mailing pieces were mailed to them first, then to those interested, a series of letters and booklets were sent, and where possible personal calls were made.

Here is a letter which was most successful in bringing inquiries for a machine selling for about $2,500.00. It was mailed to a restricted field - Public Service Companies - and it brought interested inquiries in considerable volume.

When Millions Were Actually THROWN IN THE GUTTER!

"The most expensive gutters in the world" that is what they called the canals of 1830 which cost $200,000,000 to build and were doomed by the locomotive.

What do you suppose they will call the trenches of today, where whole gangs of laborers, take days to dig up stretches of expensively paved streets, JUST TO LAY PIPES AND CABLES OR DRAINS UNDER THEM?"

"The most expensive ditches in the world" - probably. FOR THESE SAME HOLES COULD BE BORED AT A TENTH OF THE COST WITH A HYDRAUGER!

All the work of tearing up paving, all the expense of resurfacing, might just as well be thrown into the ditch, for all the need there is of it or all the good you get out of it.

You see, the HydrAuger bores UNDER the street. It can make any size hole from 2 1/4 inches to 10 1/2 inches. It can bore any length up to 120 ft. It works as fast as a foot a minute, AND IT COSTS ONLY 10 CENTS TO 30 CENTS A FOOT!

"In 1930, we made plans for installing water mains in a newly incorporated borough", writes the Richland Township Water Co. of Windber, PA, "through which passes three paved highways. Our permit was conditioned upon NOT BREAKING THE PAVED SURFACE OF THE HIGHWAY. Thirty or more crossings were necessary. The HydrAuger enabled us to do the work in 1931 at minimum expenditure. We know of no better or more economical machine for its purpose. We completed the job for less than half the estimated cost of tunneling."

We can save more than half for you, too. May we tell you how? Your name on the enclosed card will bring full information by mail, without obligation.

Sincerely, _______________

____

Letter 4 - They Said It Couldn't Be Done

HAVE YOU EVER TRIED to sell fertilizer, shrubbery and the like to suburbanites? It is not easy at the best of times, but during the depression, when you couldn't get rid of real estate for love or money, and when the mortgage companies were taking over homes right and left, selling fertilizer and such for the lawns was a real problem. Yet it was done. And here is one letter that did it with amazing success.

How To End Worries Over Scraggly Lawns

Dear Neighbor:

With your permission, I am going to make an analysis of the soil of your lawn to determine - at my own risk and expense - what elements are lacking in it, what you need for stronger, healthier, more closely grown turf.

Mind you, this will not cost you a penny or obligate you in any way. I am going to make this analysis just to show you how little is needed to correct the texture of your soil and make possible the growing of rich, thick grass.

You see, soil gets acid or alkaline such as your body does. Let your body become too acid and the results are quickly apparent in sallow skin, eruptions, disease. Let the soil of your lawn become too acid and the grass on it will quickly grow sallow, faded, full of weeds and noxious growths. But that condition can be quickly corrected - the missing elements easily added - once you have determined what the trouble is.

Will you let us make a chemical analysis of the soil in your lawn - and send you a report of it - WITHOUT COST OR OBLIGATION TO YOU? John Smith of Jamestown, VA, wrote us:

"I should never have believed it possible that so slight a changing of the treatment of the soil could so quickly rebuild and re-establish a lawn. Your analysis showed us how to work wonders with our place."

Just your name on the enclosed card will bring you a FREE chemical analysis of your soil condition, with clear directions as to just what elements are needed to supply anything now lacking. A similar analysis from any chemist would cost several dollars.

Analysis will be made in the order in which requests are received, so if you would like to get your orders quickly, please mail your card NOW or telephone.

Sincerely, ________________

Letter 5 - A 100,000 Mark Note

TO SHOW HOW READILY you can adapt to your business an idea that has been used successfully in some other line, here is an adaptation of the "Dollar Letter" (See Letter #10).

Pinned to the top of this letter was a 100,000 mark German note. Its purpose, like that of the dollar, was to get the reader's immediate attention and arouse his interest in the message of letter.

It worked so well that the Wall Street Journal, for whom the letter was written, reported that it was the most successful subscription-getter they had ever used.

Will You Accept The Enclosed German Reichsbank Note For 100,000 Marks, With Our Compliments?

Dear Sir:

If the enclosed German Reichsbank Note for 100,000 Marks pays for one minute of your time, consider yourself engaged.

Yes, it's a real Reichsbank Note, put out by the German Government. Before the War, 100,000 marks were worth $23,820.00 in our money.

But when this particular issue of notes was retired, it took 10,000,000 notes like this to get a mark worth 24 cents in gold!

That is what uncontrolled inflation did to German money. As fast as new issues were brought out, the old ones dropped in value, until a man's only chance to get ahead lay in putting his money in common stocks, or into goods or real estate -

or something that would go up in price just as fast as the value of his money went down.

In a small way, something of the kind may occur here. Even with inflation under perfect control, the value of the inflated money is bound to drop, while common stocks and goods and real estate will go up in value.

The question is - what type of stocks will depreciate most? And what effect will inflation have upon various lines of industry?

That is where the Blank Street Journal can be of genuine help to you. Its facts are not merely timely, but they are derived from original sources, and their accuracy can be depended upon. But that isn't all. The facts it brings to you each day are interpreted from the standpoint of the investor and of the business man, enabling you to invest your money or to plan your business with understanding and foresight.

The Blank Street Journal is the source of information for countless statisticians, newspapers and market services. Yet the information for which you pay the high fees is just as readily available to you in the pages of the daily Blank Street Journal, as it is to them.

The enclosed card entitles you to the next SIXTY ISSUES of the Blank Street Journal for $3. Not only that, but it brings you FREE EXAMINATION of the first five copies. If these five do not make clear to you the financial trend, if they do not show you every phase of business and financial activity, just tell us to cancel, and you will be out nothing.

Will you TRY it? Will you let us send you accurate news from the very heart of the financial center of the country NOW - when that news may be worth more to you than ever in your lifetime? Will you mail the enclosed form TODAY?

Sincerely, _______________

Letter 6 - Close Outs

END OF THE SEASON SALES are the plague of every merchant. How to clean out the remnants of stock at a price that will appeal to the public and still leave a modicum of profit is something to make any advertising man rack his brain.

Here is a letter that we used first on books. When the Simond's War History sale was over, there were a couple of thousand returned or damaged sets on hand.

The price was reduced to 25 cents and a letter along the lines of the attached was mailed. It pulled so well that the 2,000 sets were disposed of at once, and the order cost was found to be so low that it paid to deliver some 6,000 brand new sets on the orders that came in.

Adapted to Traveling Bags, the letter did just as well. Here it is, used to dispose of the odds and ends of a stock of Overcoats. It has been successful on every product on which we have used it.

790 Leftover Ulsters At A Big Discount!

Dear Sir:

In the rush and excitement of selling, in the past two months, of 21,000 "Keep Warm" Winter Ulsters - there was no time to pay attention to exactly how sizes and colors were running.

The result is that now, with the season near its end, we find ourselves with 790 coats left over - in all sizes - BUT WITHOUT A COMPLETE RANGE OF SIZES IN ANY ONE COLOR!

There are dark grays and blues and beautiful brown heather-mixtures, in Greatcoats that we sold in the past all the way up to $47.00 - really handsome colors, all of them - but we can't be sure of having your exact size in the color you specify.

And you know how the Overcoat season is - if these Ulsters are not all disposed of before Christmas, some of them will probably be on our hands until next Fall.

So rather than carry any of them over until then, we have decided to make one sweeping reduction, and offer these 790 smart, distinctive, beautifully tailored Greatcoats of fine, warm, double-texture pure wool cloth - for only $27.65!

This is the lowest price we have ever made on these all-wool "Keep Warm"

Ulster Coats. Just try to find their equal - in style, in workmanship, in fine quality material for $40 or $50.

Only 790 Coats Left We have just 790 of these double-texture all-wool Greatcoats to sell at this low price. When they are gone, your chance to save on your Winter Ulster will go with them. But while these 790 last, you can get as perfect-fitting, as good-

looking, as fine-quality a Winter Greatcoat as ever you would want to wear, at an almost unheard-of bargain.

If you will just write your name and three simple measures on the enclosed card and mail to us, we will send you a "Keep Warm" Ulster - that will exactly fit you -

by prepaid Parcel Post.

You may keep the overcoat for a full week. Then, if for ANY REASON AT ALL you don't care to keep the coat, you can send it back AT OUR EXPENSE. But if you are so well-pleased with it that you don't want to part with it, just send us $27.65, the low price at which we are offering these last remaining 790 coats.

SEND NO MONEY - simply mail the post card. But do it at once, this opportunity to save money will not occur again.

Yours up to 790,

PRESIDENT

Letter 7 - Using A Premium

WHEN YOU WANT TO LAND a fish, you bait your hook with something that the fish likes. When you want to land a lot of orders, the same principle applies.

A client wanted to sell a new, small size travelling bag. He tried selling it on its merits alone, and got 3% to 4% of orders. Since the bag sold for

$7.95, and 3% gave him an order cost of only $1, that was profitable. But he wanted volume.

So he tried using a bit of bait. To all who would send for this new bag, he offered a Fountain Pen with their name die-stamped on it in letters of gold. Instead of only 3% or 4%, that attractive bait brought the orders up to 10%, 12% and even on some lists, to 14%.

Will you accept one of the latest model, self-filling Fountain Pens with your name die- stamped in raised letters upon it - in return for a little favor I want you to do?

The courtesy is a small one, pleasant and easy to render.

For years, you know, the standard size Travelling Bag has been an 18 inch bag like the famous "Twentieth Century Bag", but lately many friends have been writing that they would like a bit smaller bag than this - something light and inexpensive, but with all the strength and fine appearance, all the unique conveniences of the "Twentieth Century".

Now we are trying one out - a bag so convenient that we don't believe its equal has ever been made before - certainly not anywhere near the price.

Every time you pack this Bag, you will be thankful for the TIME-SAVING convenience of its wonderful interior pockets. It has a place for everything you need on a trip - and it almost "packs itself".

Ever have toothpaste or shaving cream get all over your clean shirts and collars?

Or the stopper come out of a bottle and the contents run over everything?

Then you'll appreciate the convenience of the moisture-proof pockets lined with the long- wearing, high grade hospital rubber. No moisture can leak through it.

These five moisture-proof pockets will hold shaving gel, talcum powder or toilet water - all your toilet needs.

On the opposite side of the bag are two full-length pockets with folders for carrying shirts, ties, underwear, socks, and any papers that you need when you go on a trip.

These handy pockets are collapsible and take up no room when not filled. They not only enable you to pack your bag in half the time it used to take, but they keep all your things shipshape, and leave the entire bottom part of the bag free to pack suits of clothes and other large articles. A wealth of packing space.

I am writing a few of our customers for their opinion of these new Travelling Bags. We call them "RedypaktBags" because they're handy for so many different uses.

I would like you to try one of them for a week - USE it on your next trip - see how convenient, how time saving, how handsome it is. Compare it with bags you have paid $12 or $15 for. And then tell me what you and your friends think of it.

It is a small favor, but it means a great deal to me. We are thinking of making a general offering of these "RedypaktBags" all over the country, but before doing it, I would like to have your opinion.

Just your name on the enclosed card will bring a "RedypaktBag" to you to try out for a week FREE. At the end of the week, if you should like the BAG so well that you want to keep it for your own, you can have it for only $7.95. If you don't want to keep it, please send it back at my expense, telling me what you think about it, and I'll be deeply grateful to you.

Naturally, this special price holds good only if your card comes in at once, while your advice will still be of value to us.

Won't you, therefore, put your name on the card and mail it now? I thank you for your courtesy.

Gratefully yours, ______________

P.S. The new model, sell-filling fountain pen which I'll send along will have your name die-stamped upon it. And whether or not you keep the "RedypackBag", I want you to keep the pen as a present from me, entirely free of charge. It's a return for your courtesy in examining the "RedypaktBag" and giving me your opinion about it.

Letter 8 - An Indirect Approach

THE LONGEST WAY AROUND is frequently the shortest way home - when it comes to selling people an idea.

If we were to come to you, and tell you that we'd be glad to put your name in some "Who's Who" provided you would dig up $10 for a copy, you'd shy off at once. It would be too apparent that the only reason we were listing you was to get your $10.

But if we approach you tactfully and indirectly, there is a good chance we shall get both your listing and your $10. Here is an example of the indirect approach that worked well.

Dear Madam:

Would you be good enough to do me a favor? I promise not to ask too much.

You can help to solve a problem which is of significance to all officials of Women's clubs. You know that for 34 years, the leading Club Women of the United States have been recorded each year in the So & So of Women's Clubs.

This year, a symposium is being conducted among the leading officials of Women's Clubs, to determine whether it would add measurably to the So & So's value to include an entirely new section - a "Who's Who Among Club Women", giving a short biographical sketch with the offices you have held and all the outstanding achievements of your Club life.

Your Club Activities entitles you to representation in this exclusive section. Will you be good enough to give me your opinion of the value of a section?

There will be no charge for the listing, but since each listing will mean considerable additional expense in the way of typesetting and the like, we shall ask each of those whose biographical sketches appear in this "Who's Who" to subscribe for one copy of So & So. To make up for this however, we shall send it to them - not at the regular price of $5.00, but at a special pre-publication discount of 15% - making the net price to them $4.25, and even from this figure we shall give them an additional discount for advance payment.

We shall greatly appreciate an expression of your opinion from you. If that opinion is favorable, please fill out the Record attached, giving your Club connection and all those little personal items that Society Editors and others ask for, when you own or your club's activities bring your name into the news.

The enclosed envelope needs no stamp. Won't you, therefore fill out the Record NOW - while it is in your hands and mail it right back in the enclosed envelope?

Thank you!

Appreciatively, ________________

Letter 9 - Bargains

EVERYONE OFFERS BARGAINS - at least, everyone claims that if you take into consideration the quality and so on of his product, it is a bargain at this price.

But what everyone claims, no one believes. So you've got to do more than claim that your price is low or you offer an unusual bargain. You've got to show the reason why.

Here is a letter that was unusually successful in convincing readers that they were getting something unusual in the way of price reduction, and therefore brought back their orders in profitable quantities.

Mr. Business Man:

"Name your own price!" said the manufacturer.

And we did.

You know how most factories are - busy and working overtime eight or ten months of the year and idle the rest. And those idle months, like the famines of ancient Egypt, eat up most of the profits of the busy ones.

We offered to keep this factory busy making new Carozy Robes all during the idle season.

"Name your own price", was the answer.

We named a price. It was accepted without cavil or question, with the result that we can offer you, at $9.85, a Motor Rob that customers tell us could not be equalled in stores at anywhere near that price. The folder enclosed will give you some idea of the beauty and richness of this luxurious Robe.

Naturally, bargains like this won't last long. We got this one manufacturer's output for three months, but while three months' output is a lot of robes, they won't go far among our more than 300,000 customers.

The enclosed card will bring one of these beautiful new Carozy Robes to you for a week's examination - FREE! No money - no risk - no obligation. Just the postcard.

"A direct saving to me of at least $7.50," wrote John Smith of Clarksburg, WV, when he saw his robe.

The card will be worth good money to you, too, IF YOU WILL MAIL IT AT ONCE.

Yours for mutual cooperation,

PRESIDENT

Letter 10 - The Dollar Letter

HERE IS THE MOST SUCCESSFUL letter we have ever heard of - the famous "Dollar Letter". Pinned to its top was a crisp, new dollar bill - a real dollar bill.

This letter pulled better than a 90% response. The writer of this letter told us that from 175,000 mailed, he got back $270,000, plus more than 90% of the $1 bills mailed out with them.

But this was only the start. From the list of more than 150,000 people who gave that $270,000, further subscriptions were secured to the amount of nearly $14,000,000.

Dear Mr. Jones:

Here's a dollar: Yes, it's a REAL dollar - nice and clean and new.

Keep it if you want to, after you've read this letter - but I don't believe you will, then.

Here's what it's all about:

I've made an investment of a thousand dollars in human nature - human kindness. I've mailed a thousand dollars - in a thousand letters to a thousand people picked at random. I have done this because I believe that every one is really kind, way down inside - that no one is REALLY heartless and that the only reason why folks do not help where help is needed is just because these needs are not IMPRESSED upon them hard enough.

"And that's the mission of each of my thousand dollars - to impress the importance of a need. This thousand dollars is my subscription to the Blank Hospital - and I'm investing in the belief that every one will bring back several more - at least another - with it. So our subscription - which I'm starting in this way will be at least two thousand - maybe five - for there's going to be a lot of you who will send a five or a ten or more - when you mail my dollar back.

Remember - both my dollar and your dollars go to help crippled children.

Will EVERY ONE come back?

Will everyone bring something more?

Are people really kind - or REALLY heartless?

Have I made a good investment?

What is YOUR answer?

Sincerely, _____________

Letter 11 - Selling Securities By Mail

HOW ABOUT SELLING STOCKS by mail? Millions of dollars of such sales have been made, and when properly done, it is one of the least expensive methods of selling known.

The easiest way, of course, is to send an inexpensive letter to your list first, to find out who can be interested in that particular type of investment. To those who answer that letter, you can afford to send a whole series of follow-ups, booklets or make a personal call.

Here is a type of letter which has met with marvelous success in offers of this kind.

Here Is The Industry That Started

MANY OF THE GREAT FORTUNES OF TODAY!

Dear Sir:

Men made iron and steel for thousands of years. Along came a new process and a man named Carnegie to capitalize it, and made a thousand millionaires. When "in steel" while this magic change was in process, made fortunes almost overnight.

Men have been brewing beer for thousands of years. Along came Prohibition and practically closed the industry. Breweries were dismantled, their working crews scattered to the four winds.

BUT NOW, WITH A STROKE OF THE PEN, PRESIDENT ROOSEVELT HAS CHANGED ALL THIS. NOW, ALMOST OVERNIGHT, COMES A DEMAND FOR BEER GREATER THAN THE COUNTRY HAS EVER BEFORE KNOWN!

The stocks of the few active, well-equipped breweries soared overnight. In two weeks, they increased 48% in value, while the average of all stocks went up only 6%. Yet if the record of earnings means anything, that is only the start. Men with good brewery stocks should see them rise to almost phenomenal heights as did those "in steel" back in Carnegie's day. Breweries today should make even more.

Yet there is one brewery which has been in continuous operation in the same family for 77 years, with a splendid plant and a fine old name, and which has so far escaped the notice of stock market investors. To us, it seems to offer greater possibilities of profit from small investment than anything you can put your money into today.

May we tell you more about it?

Sincerely, ________________

Letter 12 Securing Inquiries For A Booklet

HOW CAN YOU MOST EASILY find the people interested in new courses, new sets of books and the like?

By offering to the most likely lists of prospects, to send without cost a booklet of interest only to people desiring that particular type of knowledge. The encyclopedia Britannica, for instance offers a booklet containing sample pages and illustrations from its new Encyclopedia. Collier's offers a booklet telling in the words of Dr. Eliot of Harvard what he considers the essentials of a liberal education, and thus finds the people who can be interested in Dr. Eliot's Five Foot Shelf of Books.

Here is such a letter, designed to winnow out from the other lists the names of all those interested in learning the art of Public Speaking. It is one of the most successful inquiry- bringing letters we have used.

Now For The First Time

- THE SECRET OF EFFECTIVE SPEECH -

FREE!

Dear Sir:

At your request, I shall be glad to send you one of the most talked-of little books ever written. It will cost you exactly one cent - the price of the stamp that will bring the enclosed card back to me.

The name of this booklet is - "The Secret of Effective Speech". The principal part of it was written by perhaps the most successful speaker of modern times, the man who made over $4,000,000.00 from his lectures, and then used it to send young men through College - Russell Conwell, author of "Acres of Diamonds".

The Secret of Effective Speech should be read by every executive who ever has to face a hostile audience, whether that audience consists of one man or a thousand.

It is not made up of rules and principles, but of the few common-sense essentials which Conwell found of most importance in his thousands of appearances on the public platform. It is radical. It is stimulating. AND IT IS FREE!

Your name and address on the enclosed card will bring you a copy of "The Secret of Effective Speech", with out compliments. You will like this little book. It

is short, but there is a tremendous lot in it. Every time you read it, you will realize more clearing why Russell Conwell had so many thousand enthusiastic admirers, who audiences hung upon his every word.

Frankly, we are taking this means of bringing to the attention of a few alert business executives a new method of teaching Public Speaking - a method so striking and simple, yet so amazingly successful, that it is taking the country by storm.

Will you use the postcard NOW - TODAY?

Sincerely, _______________

Letter 13 - Sports Appeal, Sales Appeal

SPORTS ARTICLES ARE notably successful in mail selling, where you can get lists of people interested in any particular sport. Fishing tackle, golf clubs and balls, tennis racquets and a host of other products have been successfully sold by mail.

There is even a concern in Baltimore which sells fine saddlery by mail and has built a surprisingly profitable business.

Here is a letter that sold Field Glasses by mail, and sold them in goodly quantities. Its basic idea is just as applicable to dozens of other products that appeal to all sportsmen.

Now the Far Distances are Yours

WITH MAGIC EYES THAT SEE FOR MILES!

Dear Friend:

Here is a wonderful way to add to the enjoyment of your trips, to give you "ring side" seats at every sporting event, to bring anything you want to see within a few feet of you MULTIPLYING YOUR OWN EYE-SIGHT BY THE POWER OF THESE EIGHT MAGIC LENSES!

Four-Mile Eyes - that is what they give you, spanning distances like the fabled seven- league boots of childhood. For the hunter, they are a necessity. For the tourist or traveler, they add a zest that doubles the enjoyment of sightseeing. For those who love sports, they make a nearby window or hilltop as desirable as the most expensive "ring side" seat.

Yet for a little while, they can be had FOR LESS THAN THE COST OF A SINGLE SEAT!

You see, the finest glasses in the world are made in Central Europe. And you know how conditions have been over there - many highly skilled artisans getting lenses for a month's toil than they would for a single day's work here. The result?

Bargains as you will never get again. Bargains such as we never dreamed of being able to offer in Fine Field Glasses. Prices are higher over there now and are stiffening rapidly, but up to a few weeks ago, you could get the finest achromatic day and night lenses at figures so ridiculously low as to seem like a gift.

We had a lot of extra powerful Officer's Field Glasses shipped to us at those prices a month ago. They have just been unpacked and gone over, and they are beauties. Filled with specially large achromatic day and night lens, and equipped with compass and focusing scale. They are the most powerful glasses of the kind we have ever seen at anywhere near the price.

I have a pair on my desk before me as I write, and through them I can mount the high tension wires on a hill a couple of miles east of here, and through these glasses, I can watch every move of the builders. If they were football players, I could see them better than from the choicest seat.

And the reason? These glasses were made for the use of Army Officers, and they had to be good. They are the only 8-lens Galilean Field Glass with compass and leather case that sell for less than $30.00! But while they last, I am going to let you have a pair for $7.95!

Not only that, but if you mail the enclosed card right away, I will send them to you, postpaid, for a week's FREE EXAMINATION and TRIAL!

SEND NO MONEY! Just your name and address on the enclosed card will bring a pair of these extra-powerful, *-lens Officer's Field Glasses to you at our risk, our expense, TRY them! Test them against the finest glasses you can find selling at $30.00 to $40.00 a pair. If these are not clear, stronger, more satisfactory in every way, send them back. If you are willing to part with them for any reason, send them back. Otherwise, $7.95 makes them your own, an endless source of pleasure and usefulness. On that understanding, will you TRY a pair of these Magic Eyes? With that distinct agreement, will you put your name on the enclosed card, and mail it NOW?

You will never have another such opportunity.

Sincerely, ________________

Letter 14 - Using Pressure

WANT TO START A BUSINESS of your own by mail? Here is a letter that brought in more than $1,000,000.00 worth of orders for a new concern in its first six months.

Every man wants to make money. Every man wants to see his money grow.

When you start by asking your reader if he'd like to see one dollar grow to a hundred, you have his attention. when you prove to him that he can learn how to work such a miracle before he pays out a single penny, you are sure of his interest. After that, the bringing back of the actual order is mere detail.

This letter is high-pressure... too much so for many projects - but for those that can stand it, it embodies every feature of the successful selling letter.

My dear Sir:

Would you like to see $1.00 grow to $60.00 - $8.00 grow to $500.00 by next March?

Let me tell you how:

I am going to send you within the next few days a set of seven little books. These books are probably not like any you have ever seen before because:

They are about YOU!

They show you that you have been using but a small part of your real abilities -

that back in your subliminal mind", as the scientists call it, is a sleeping Giant who. awakened, can carry you on to fame and fortune almost overnight! A Genie-

of-your-Brain as powerful, as capable of satisfying your every wish, as was ever Aladdin's wonderful Genie-of-the- lamp of old.

They make your Day Dreams, your visions of wonderful achievement, of fortune, health and happiness COME TRUE - not five, ten, or fifteen years from now, but TODAY, A.D. 1925!

I am going to send these little books to you - with no obligations on your part - for you to read and ACTUALLY TRY OUT for a week at my risk and expense.

But - there's just one thing - I don't want to send these without first getting your permission. You can grant that in a moment on the enclosed special "Courtesy Card".

When I send the books, there's absolutely no obligation on your part to pay for them. You can return them for ANY reason, or for no reason at all.

BUT HERE'S THE MOST IMPORTANT PART!

If you; find these little books are everything I say about them (and you're to be the sole judge), how much would you expect to pay for them? $30.00? $50.00?

$100.00? That's what ordinary courses, which merely promise to show you how to do some special kind of work, cost you. Certainly, if this one will do the half of what I've promised you, it will be worth all of that - and more!

Well - if you decide to keep these books, you need send me - NOT $50.00 or $100.00, not even their regular price of $13.50 - but my

SPECIAL INTRODUCTORY PRICE TO YOU, good only on this ADVANCE EDITION of $6.85! (If you prefer the more convenient monthly payments, send only $1.00 a month for eight months.) And that isn't all!

If within 6 months your $1.00 hasn't grown to $60.00 - if you can't credit to the $6.85 you pay for this Course at least $500.00 of ADDITIONAL EARNINGS -

send back the books and I'll refund to you cheerfully and in full every cent you have paid to me for them.

There are no conditions - no strings attached of any kind to this offer. If within 6 months these little books have not brought you the pot of gold at the foot of the rainbow, then they are not for you. Send them back and get your money!

Letter 15 - Using The "You" Element

THERE IS A CONCERN in one of the Eastern states which built a business running into the millions on four letters. Those four letters were used over and over again, year after year. They finally wore out, but after several years' rest, they are again good for an occasional mailing.

All those letters were built around the most important and interesting subject you can write about to any reader - HIMSELF.

Here is the most successful of these four letters - "Will you give me a little information about YOURSELF?"

Dear Sir:

Will you give me a little information about yourself - just your height and weight?

I want to send you one of our famous "Rainproof" Coats (designed especially for substantial Business Men) for you to examine, free of charge; but I can't send one in your size without knowing your height and weight.

Over 36,000 Men-of-Affairs, in all parts of the country, wear these "Rainproof"

Coats on rainy days. They are just the kind of coat EVERY well-dressed business man needs in the Spring and Fall, for they are really TWO COATS IN ONE - a perfect raincoat for stormy days and a well-appearing Topcoat for cold and windy days.

More than 36,000 keen business and professional men who have ordered "Rainproof" Coats during the past two years paid us prices varying from $17.85 to $23.50 for their coats.

NOW FOR ONE MONTH ONLY - WE ARE OFFERING THESE "RAINPROOF"

COATS AT THE LOWEST PRICE AT WHICH THEY HAVE BEEN OFFERED IN THE TWO YEARS - $16.65!

From Ohio, Mr. John Jones,

Vice-President and Treasurer of Blank Cement Co., writes:

"I never got as much comfort and satisfaction out of any coat as I have from the "Rainproof". I had been looking for such a garment for years - a coat I could wear on all occasions and be proud of."

And this is just one out of hundreds of letters and telegrams that have come from men who have ordered these "Rainproof" Coats and been delightedly surprised with their fine style, great usefulness and good value.

Won't you fill in your height and weight on the enclosed postcard, and mail it to me? Then I can send you one of these famous "Rainproof" Coats - in your exact size by Parcel Post for a week's FREE TRIAL. You can examine the coat at your leisure, with no insisting clerks at your side, and WEAR IT A FULL WEEK FREE.

If you don't think it is just the kind of coat you've always wanted, just fire it back at MY EXPENSE, and accept my thanks for the privilege of sending it to you.

But remember - this is the only month in which we are going to offer "Rainproof"

Coats a the special "lowest-in-years' price of $14.65!

Hadn't you better drop the postcard into the mail RIGHT NOW - while you can take advantage of this Special Offer?

What This Series Has To Do With You in our Modern Age

Preamble

LET'S LAY OUT SOME basics.

When you understand marketing and copywriting, *you can achieve, acquire, and accomplish <u>anything</u> you want – by helping everyone around you get what <u>they</u> want.* That's why this book was created – to help you do just that.

People are living a story that they are very serious about, for the most part. They think they have no choice in this matter. People actually choose by their many decisions – all day long, for all their lives.

What they don't understand, mostly, is that story they are living is being created by them and lasts as long as they want it to.

Your job as a marketer or copywriter, accept it or not, is to help them with their story by describing offers to them that they can use to push their story along.

The reason for this series of books is to bring you a collection of stories lived by some of the world's greatest copywriters and sales-persons. When you study their stories, you'll then understand how marketing is actually done – not the way it's been sold as a subject since just before the Internet was invented.

Humankind hasn't changed much, if any, since we started writing down our histories. Our markets are the same as when they were bazaars in the local village square. What people want hasn't changed, their motivations haven't changed. Only our current circumstances.

Most people believe the metaphor that we are each on a journey through the life we live out on this planet. High-tech or primitive, the basic human reactions are the same as they always have been, regardless of what we encounter on this journey.

The idea of a journey-story is what starts to tie up all the loose ends of marketing into a cohesive approach – an underlying system which explains all, resolves all. If you understand what motivates every person on Earth, then you can form your offer to help them along on that journey they are on. And they'll pay you well for this – which helps you on your own journey.

Life-journeys were defined years ago by a professor named Joseph Campbell. He wrote several books about how there is one common plot to all myths and legends. Campbell found that the stories which resonated through history, that were retold time and time again, were the ones which fit a certain pattern.

Campbell told of this story as a journey which every hero (or heroine) undertook. And this common journey-story can be as complicated or as simple as you'd like.

The very simplest is this:

Departing on the Journey

- The call to adventure, perhaps rejected at first

- Meeting a mentor or guide.

- Point of no Return, where the world transforms

Life-Changes

- A series of trials, temptations, and resolutions

- Atonement and rebirth – *total* paradigm shift

- Goal achievement

Returning

- Flight with the goal-solution

- Rescue by companions

- Recrossing back into normal life with new freedoms

The common players in every story:

- Hero or Heroine

- Helpers

- Goal or object being attained.

Marketers do their pitch to help a person along at one stage or another of their journey. Pitches all aren't all calls to adventure. You are offering products which symbolize something that is vital to that journey progress. Your pitch is another helper for whatever they are facing. It's up to you to know your potential customer or client to see what they need so you can fill it.

As you study Campbell (recommended) and those who wrote about him (Chris Vogler has a good study in this area) you'll see this above description is pretty watered down. I've kept it simple so you can apply it in our "non-heroic" times.

It is the single story which is told over and over, regardless of circumstance. While there are as many variations as there are individuals on this planet, the basic plot is the same for everyone.

This is what I found to be the common thread through all Marketing and copywriting as well. If you go back to find the all-time great advertisements and marketing campaigns, you'll see that they tell a story.

- *"Do You Make These Mistakes in English?"*

- *"They laughed when I sat down at the piano – but when I began to play..."*

- *"At 60 miles an hour the loudest noise in this new Rolls-Royce comes from the electric clock."*

These are stories which sold over and over. Why? Because they help a person on their journey.

The products they buy are symbols which help them on their journey. Clothes tell the status of a person, they are the costume which helps that person get into or stay in character during the journey. Vehicles, electronic gadgets, houses – all these things make the journey easier or are tools which make that achievement possible.

You also have the reverse – where people are desperately working to avoid the journey in front of them, and seek continual distraction from what they know to be true.

The copywriter or marketer who knows these and a few other facts will be able to make sense of all the various "schools" and "brands" of marketing, as well as all the "guru-speak" which is out there.

What follows next are a few short essays which expand on this concept. I've left them as originally written – some of the points repeat what I've just told you. All I'm telling you here is simply a metaphor, a tool-set. Do with it what you will.

Test all this for yourself and throw away everything which doesn't work for you. Only then will you be able to use it effectively in your own marketing.

What Story are YOU Living?

PEOPLE LIVE IN THEIR own story. And that story controls their life.

People are preoccupied with that story – how it will turn out, plot twists, happy or tragic ending, their story that runs their life. They listen to this story more than they listen to the people who are trying to talk to them in real life.

And, as the old phrase, they write their story as they go along, much as Shakespeare would write the play even as the actors rehearsed it.

People get their inspiration for that story from the other stories around them.

Their story is continually running in every person's head, constantly refined and improved by the stories they compare with it.

This comparing is what can get people into trouble. Or saves their bacon. It's truly a life or death scene from day to day. This explains the drama so many people go through, while others lead calm and cheerful lives. It's the story-line they follow.

People are in search of the perfect story. One that explains their life so far and gives them direction to follow.

The person who influences their story controls them - by their own choice. Any politician knows this. The really effective ones (like FDR, and similar) leave a feel-good "legacy" which takes decades to unravel the factual truth from the fictional story they wove. (The Great Depression was made worse and longer than it should have been.)

The bad politicians (Hitler, Mussolini, Stalin) weren't bad because of what they did (well, yes - but that's another story.) Let me rephrase that: They weren't bad *according to the people in their own country* – even for years after they were driven from power – because they consistently told a story which with their people wanted.

Hitler was going to return Germany to a level of prominence in the world that was unjustly taken away from them, back to global approval.

Some people in Russia even today long for a return to the "good old days" of Stalin and complete control over their lives – stable security.

People live a certain story in their life.

They compare the stories they hear and see with that internal story to see if they are living their life the right way - are they following the plot right, are they being the right character?

So when you tell a good story, you get elected. If you keep telling a good story (like FDR's "it was all the earlier guy's fault...") then people continue to like you and you stay in power. That's why U.S. Presidents are limited to two terms ever since.

Some people can tell a story too well for our own good.

Seriously. That's the way things are.

But let's back up.

I'm not counting on you believing me. In fact, I'm counting on you disbelieving me. Because until you start listening to the stories around you with a critical ear and eye, you will continue to live a life which takes all the money you make and leaves you nothing in return (except some expensive doo-dads, bumper stickers and yard signs.)

The old saying is true: out of 100 people graduating, 5 will retire wealthy, 10 will be able to retire at all, and the rest will be broke and dependent on the government or charity to keep them alive.

The difference is their story and who they let influence its outcome.

We aren't here to talk about politics. (It's just that they make such good punching bags, er... examples - when they are no longer around.)

The only difference between the people writing the ads which make you buy their stuff and the speech writers that make you vote for a certain young, good-looking politician is... Nothing.

They both use your emotions to get what THEY want.

Not what YOU want.

Yes, you have it all rationalized out that you did the right thing. But funny enough, when enough things break on that gorgeous chunk of metal in your driveway - you'll trade it in for another of the same brand.

The really good marketers find out what you want and offer it to you in a way that's natural for you to accept. The great copywriters hep you live your life the way you already think you want it.

People disagree on who the all-time legendary copywriters are. There are huge long lists of people you've never heard of, and how these people were Kings of their Heaps.

What I've done is to take all these lists and boil them down the the same few names which keep coming up.

Then I've studied *those* authors to see what they said worked for them - and found a few *other* authors to study.

Meanwhile, I took the same key datums all these authors said and boiled them down. (And decided to reproduce those I could as the simplest way of getting these books to you – in its own series.)

The final step was to boil even those down until when the steam cleared, there was just one nugget left in the bottom of that huge pot.

You've already been introduced to it:

Life is a journey-story.

The person can only figure out if their story is a good one if they compare it to other stories around them.

People who tell them stories which are similar to theirs can get them to do what they want.

This is called copywriting.

It is part of a subject called "marketing" - which is really just communication.

People who are known as "good talkers" or "good salespeople" or "great communicators" are all just marketing their own story in a way people want to hear it.

When you buy their stuff (or vote their way) you've decided that your story would be better if you took the action they told you to.

We are going to get to the main way these people get away with ordering you around.

But all these copywriters and speech writers know one thing:

Your life-story is built from emotion.

In fact, all communication is built from emotion. Every word has some emotional connotation by itself, weak or strong. They draw their power from the words on either side. This is what gives poetry it's strength — and why Shakespeare is still so powerful, even though no one speaks that version of English these days.

Every good story involves you emotionally in the outcome. You sit in that theater, or in front of that TV, or in a "good" book - completely oblivious to everything around you - until it ends.

And then for days afterwards, you are still hearing that story go around in your thoughts.

If they told you a good enough story, you will hear it for years. You'll even change your life so that you are constantly reminded of their story by the various doo-dads you have around you.

It's not just buying the book or DVD or downloading that TED talk. (Or for some, playing that game over and over and over until you figure out how to win all the levels - or until the next version comes out...)

It's the story in it. Something in their story makes you want to have that outcome in your own story.

The emotions they used to tell their story is one you like to experience. So you keep coming back over and over.

Or you buy their products over and over. Or vote for that party over and over. Or watch that actor or actress over and over.

You have become one of the highest prizes. You're a client. Also known as a devoted fan.

But all is good. *All* stories are good ones.

Because you are just following your emotions. And you're always right.

That's the way you and I and everyone are wired.

Practically no one is immune. Well, statistically, it's between one in a million and one in ten billion. Those people are called "enlightened" and not much marketing works on them. (They already have everything they could ever need or want anyway - but that's another story.)

What you are probably wanting to know next is: how do I learn to write like this? Or - how do I learn to write my own story?

What's The Difference Between A Good And Bad Copywriter?

I WAS WANDERING AROUND reading tons of material on writing sales pages, landing pages, scripts. I was studying headlines, subheadings, bullet points. I was absorbing the details of graphics and type-styles and colors.

I was trying to absorb all these details about the perfect marketing approach - and it was going nowhere. Just filling up my hard-drives and filling up my book-cases.

But I thought the next book or video or webinar would tell me the key point I was missing.

Bob Bly was the one to finally bust my balloon.

He said it was simple:

A good copywriter gets the sale.

Joe Sugarman said the same thing. So did most of the others when you look for it.

All these details about how to build the sales page were only valuable if they helped the ad do that one thing.

Some ad that is considered good copywriting helps the reader buy. More than just "wanting" to buy - they actually buy the stuff being talked about.

A good copywriter will make the person buy—by pushing the right emotional buttons.

The whole point of copywriting is to get the person to act. To take out their credit card and buy whatever is being talked about.

A good copywriter tells the story that reader wants to hear.

Yes, we see a problem with this.

How do you keep someone like Hitler getting in charge again?

Practically, the only way you can do this is like the joke:

Q. *How do you get down from an elephant?*

A. *You don't. You get down from a goose.*

Get it? *Goose down.*

You change the world by changing your own story.

You can proof yourself up against those who only want you following their story. Then you can decide if it's somewhere you want to go.

Reading this and deciding for yourself if it works for you is the one way you can take charge over your own story.

I'll give you a lot of other books you can read, mostly about copywriting. The rest is up to you.

The next question is almost the same:

How do you start telling stories which will help people around you to live better lives?

And that is what the good copywriters are doing every day, with every ad or article.

They are telling people stories which enable them to take action and make their own life better in some way.

You see, good copywriting makes people feel better - and act.

Bad copywriting makes people feel worse - and act.

Poor copywriting doesn't get a person to act either way. And usually isn't read after the headline.

There are good emotions and bad emotions. Either type can get a person to act.

Constantly following bad emotions will wreck your life, however. This is why people who are constantly critical have few true friends.

Critical people look for stories which have a critical storyline in them. Because they need reasons to explain the actions they take.

People decide emotionally and excuse it logically.

Good copywriting will give the logical explanation for buying. These are known as "features." But the person decides to buy based on the "benefits" which are always emotional.

Perry Marshall is known for a phrase, "Nobody who bought a drill actually wanted a drill, they wanted a hole."

(He isn't the first one to notice it, but he's the one known for saying it.)

"Wanting" is emotional. And there is some sort of emotion behind and before that "want."

You want a hole because

• people will look up to you,

• you'll have better control in your life,

• it will make you a more secure future,

• you'll finally be part of an exclusive group,

• etc.

• etc.

Meanwhile, you buy that expensive drill you are going to use once or twice and store in your shop for years later. Like most power tools owned by consumers. (Professionals are different - they'll own several. Some are called "backups.")

As you read down the sales page, you'll go through all the emotional reasons for buying, and then they'll tell you the logical reasons why you're right.

Right down to the P.S. - which tells you again to buy that item right now.

Valuable Copywriters Are Different.

VALUABLE COPYWRITERS are there to improve their own lives by improving the lives of people they talk to.

They are not good copywriters or bad copywriters - they are not poor, if they are valuable to others.

People will follow you to the end of the earth if you are consistently handing out valuable stuff.

While value is just a matter of perception, there is an underlying principle older than written history which haunts copywriters who try to short-cut this process:

You can't get without giving. You'll only *get* according to what you *give*.

This is known as the "Golden Rule" - among other things.

Zig Ziglar said it this way, *"You can get all you want in life if you help enough other people get what they want."*

Look this over carefully.

People run their lives by emotion. So a person who is able to influence their emotions can take over running all these lives. Or so some people think.

Actually, you can only get and keep a following if you are always giving valuable stuff out.

Yes, they'll pay you ungodly sums for this stuff.

But only if it's valuable - and continues to be so.

Even if you talk to other people's emotions - you'll only get what you give out. To the degree you honestly help others is the degree you'll get the help you need.

Right about now is the point where you realize I'm ruining everything.

Because from here on out, you are going to see through all the sales pages you read, all the commercials you hear or watch, every story you pick up.

You're going to look to see whether that person is giving something that's actually valuable. To you.

You're going to pull back the curtains and watch that "Wizard of Oz" do their stuff.

Doesn't mean you aren't going to buy. But it does mean what you will be in better control over what you buy and the actual "why" you are buying.

Doesn't mean you aren't emotionally involved.

But it does mean that you are going to start writing your own story.

How do you tell what's a "good" story?

Again, you're looking for the "goose down."

Work it backwards:

• You're trying to succeed every day you live.

• The storyline you are following has certain goals to be successful.

• Some activities and people you meet won't help you make your goals.

• You'll attract what you need to achieve those goals (or get what you want) by helping others achieve similar goals.

How A Story "Works"

THERE ARE MANY, MANY forms of stories. They are called by many names - "meme", legend, icon, quest, journey...

A story works because of the emotion it contains and how its presented.

This is the sole reason for the success of bestseller books, movies, songs, brands.

Sole reason.

Stories are alive to the degree they allow people to participate in the emotion they hold. Stories grow as people spread them.

Stories are tuned, like any music or instrument, to reach a certain audience, wide or narrow.

They become a "classic" when they are tuned so that generations later they are still being told – even though the language and even their model has changed.

Shakespeare's "Romeo and Juliet" became West Side Story. The Gospel of Jesus has continued to reach wide audiences in all the various ways it's been told – more recently, "The Robe," "The Greatest Story Ever Told," and "The Passion of the Christ" are several notable recent ones. Wikipedia lists 29 English ones, and five other languages.

Christopher Vogler wrote one of the best guidebooks to understanding Joseph Campbell's works. Called "The Writer's Journey," it tells how successful films were created (the "Star Wars" series for one) based on that singular "monomyth" plot.

In the introduction to the Third Edition, he also points out that a "tuned" story will actually create a physical response in the body:

I learned... to listen to my body as a judge of a story's effectiveness. I realized that the good stories were affecting the organs of my body in various ways, and the really good ones were stimulating more than one organ. An effective story grabs your gut, tightens your throat, makes your heart race and your lungs pump, brings tears to your eyes or an explosion of laughter to your lips. If I wasn't getting some kind of physiological reaction from a story, I knew it was only affecting me on an intellectual level and therefore it would probably leave audiences cold.

Vogler then went on to write an entire chapter on that very subject at the end of that edition.

Stories are that powerful.

Marketing stories which were well-crafted have won awards even through they sold no product. The industry award for advertising, the Clio, used to have this "curse" attached to it – agencies which had won the award were usually not in business by the following year.

You have to tell your marketing story in the way that gets _action_.

Bottom line.

Emotions are used to forward that goal. People "think" with their emotions, true. But no ad is worth anything to anyone unless it achieves and improves sales.

Wherever you are influencing people to continue with their journey-story, you have to end up actually getting them to do something.

This is when the story "works."

When Is a (Marketing) Story "Sensible?"

WHEN IT BALANCES LOGIC and emotion.

Let's jump way out there: There is no time, there is only Now. (This is the core secret hidden in plain site in all philosophies, if you dig far enough.) And we keep track of incidents that make up our "time-track" in order to make sense of what we are doing Now.

This is why any two people don't see the same accident in front of them. They both are recording and accepting the recording which balances both their logic and their emotion.

This is why history is constantly being re-written – by historians and individuals.

History is never pat, set, or definite. Like the old saying, "the only thing constant is change."

What "makes sense" is when you have that balance of logic and emotion.

Emotion is created. It literally means "move out." It isn't perception, it's your own patterned response to what you see or hear, or taste, etc.

Feelings are a closer description of what you perceive. Of course, that's booby-trapped by our language as well.

Mostly, you can only feel stuff that happens to you. You can feel peace. You can feel happy. You can feel good. Most feelings, if not all, are nouns, not verbs.

The one exception that comes to mind is "love". You can feel love, and you can love someone else.

But there's a trick to that word. It's not a feeling or emotion. It *creates* feelings and emotions. Love is creation. This again is one of these oldest traditions from pre-history beliefs.

Love even created hate.

Hate is only an emotion. It's out-facing. You can hold onto hate, even "hate" yourself – but the meaning just means "trying to destroy."

But in this universe, nothing is truly destroyed. Only Love can dissolve things back to their original elements.

Look back on your own life and you should be able to find enough examples of this to prove it to yourself.

Hate and negative emotions only work to physically re-arrange the shape of things around you. They'll make someone sick instead of healing them. They'll wreck relationships instead of building them.

Negative emotions are never sensible. Because they're too emotional.

Before we go too far down this line, let me point out that feelings are also created – by Love.

Love makes sense more times than not. Of course you can have a head-over-heels "true love" which won't logically make much sense. However, the people who work to make sense out of this will create a new world where their attraction to each other does make sense – and the new world they create (as long as they continue to create it) will be in perfect harmony and give them all the success they want.

IN SALES COPYWRITING, you have to achieve this balance.

People will decide emotionally and justify logically.

Your sales copy has to enable the reader to become the hero of the piece.

Hero's make sense out of nonsensical situations.

They triumph over evil to create a new reality.

Study Joseph Campbell's various books ("Hero With a Thousand Faces", "The Power of Myth") and you'll see that all the myths, legends, psychologies, and stories through the ages really boil down to a single plot (sequence).

It's this plot which also runs through all copywriting. Well, all *good* copywriting.

Bad copywriting doesn't tell a complete story or get even close.

You get involved with some simple ad and then they pitch something which is unrelated.

They are talking about a hero surviving a war, and then try to have you buy a refrigerator.

Because those copywriters don't understand what they are doing. They think they do. And they get some sales to prove it. But what they are doing is only repeating something they saw somewhere else and changing it.

Not improving it – changing it.

They don't understand how to make something make sense.

Heroes decide and act emotionally. But think logically. It will always be a surprise.

Logic isn't surprising, usually. Emotions aren't surprising. But the solution which is sensible can be very surprising.

This is your (the reader's) "Ah-ha!" moment.

And that is where the sale is made.

Because that is where they decide to act.

When it makes perfect sense.

Versions of AIDA – the Song Sung Forever.

AIDA MEANS ATTRACT, Interest, Desire, Action.

There are as many versions of this as there are fish in the ocean.

They all sing the same song with different verses. But the hero always wins.

When you take apart the conventional sales page, it's just the Hero's Journey again:

Call to Adventure – Threshold – Transformation – Return

- or -

1. Adventure Invitation (Headline)
2. Threshold is passed (Subheading, emotional benefits, "USP")
3. Hero is transformed (logical reasons, features, objections answered)
4. Hero Returns with a Gift (CTA)

Bob Bly had it this way:

The successful ad...

1. Gains attention
2. Focuses on the customer
3. Stresses benefits
4. Differentiates you from the competition
5. Proves its case
6. Establishes credibility
7. Builds value
8. Closes with a call to action

Victor Schwab wrote this over 70 years ago:

1. Get Attention

2. Show People An Advantage

3. Prove It

4. Persuade People To Grasp This Advantage

5. Ask For Action

These are all the same, really.

Just telling a story people want to hear.

And the success of that sales story is how well the copywriter tells it.

You need to know *why* as well as *how* to write good copy.

That's what this book is here for.

A good engineer bases his designs on proved principles, but listens to his intuition, too. The Wright Brothers combining their bicycle weight-lightening principles with aerodynamics they learned as children sledding – were able to get their machines off the ground with the inefficient motors of that day.

Copywriters won't just copy other's work, but will understand why these worked and then convert that success to their own product-push.

For me, once I was finally persuaded that I needed to learn this material to really make my sales take off, I then found myself surrounded by wannabe's – who were simply parroting people who had done the in-depth training in this subject.

I learned early to follow those people who had tested what actually produced sales and then slightly varied the text to see if this could be tweaked.

From this we got "*Do You Make These Mistakes in English?*" which ran for 40 years. And "*They laughed when I sat down at the piano – but when I began to play...*" which ran for 20 years. Also, this modern one: "*At 60 miles an hour the loudest noise in this new Rolls-Royce comes from the electric clock.*"

Proved headlines, copy, pitches. That's what you should be studying. Not just having huge "swipe files" you can copy and use. Because they won't do you any good until you actually know how they work.

AIDA is a song which was known to the bazaar merchants in times before history. The successful ones anyway.

To learn to sing this song effectively, you need to study those who studied why.

Are You Really Real?

THE WORST FAILURES and best successes I've seen were those where the story matched up - or didn't – with the writer-teller.

You can read these Internet Marketing pitches and wonder how they made all this money they claimed. Because they're selling junk – over and over and over.

Sure, most of them don't really make it big.

But I was studying someone who had actually made himself a huge hit in his industry. Said to be an expert on copywriting. Yet he really didn't know what he was doing. Made millions. Almost accidentally.

His real story was more interesting than the one he pitched.

Because it was real.

Yes, there are flukes out there. People who get rich when there was no reason they did – or the rules were changed later so no one could really follow their model and make the same success.

So his name isn't one of the ones to study.

He's the realest fake I've seen. And almost lost the millions he'd made. (He met an advisor to saved his money. But couldn't save his marriage.)

And when you tear apart his sales pitches to find out why they're successful – you'll see that they follow "the pattern", but have gaping holes in them.

They aren't stories you could follow. Because he told his own rag-to-riches story of bringing one book to a bunch of marketers where the whole industry didn't have a clue. And people followed him, bought his book, because it was definite and preached success.

He was determined to succeed. He persisted. After a dozen years, he became an "overnight" success. The idea he pitched was that he had become a millionaire in a little over 1 ½ years.

But he didn't. It took him a couple of decades of persistently learning from failures. He wasn't being honest. Unreal.

When you tear apart his book, it's filled with partial truths – not those which would make anyone but him actually rich.

Because he wasn't really interested in making others rich, just himself.

When you see someone who is arrogant, and preaches arrogance as a success route, you know he's ready to fail and take you with him. Because arrogance won't make any long-term success.

Success is built on making everyone around you successful. Ray Kroc (McDonald's) and Sam Walton (Wal-Mart) made more people into millionaires than they could count. So did Napoleon Hill.

They aren't the only ones. You can just see their backstory easier.

Being the best of the best – and not letting anyone else shine as bright as you – is the sure route to failure.

When you can take a person apart and see the brilliant facade built on fakery – that's when you know that everyone that person mentions is just another fake.

You'll also see that those referenced guys are also fakes.

Blind leading the blind. And you can't trust anything they say.

What you'll see written here is from the people who honestly want to help you succeed.

"Accidental Millionaires who lose it all" is not what we want to study. "Millionaires who make millionaires" is.

Real is being useful. Real is making sense.

Building a backstory from deceit won't make a solid foundation for any business.

Really real is being transparent down to your core and giving away far more value than you actually sell in goods.

The Golden Rule works all the time, all day (and night) long. How you treat others is how you'll be treated. Keep looking down on people from "on-high" based on a false route no one else can follow - and you'll eventually and rightfully be shown up as a fake.

Money made by selling drugs which ruin people's lives won't stay with you. Any criminal is ultimately brought to justice – by their own hands.

Here's the secret that made this one person rich:

In any area, you can sell more training than you can anything else.

Because most people won't carry through on your lessons – and will be buying book after book, course after course, webinar after webinar.

That's where the real money is. That's what made this guy rich.

When you read this guy's book, you see him tell this right in the pages and his videos about it.

But he's not the only one. There are several fakes in the industry he came from.

The reason: that industry (multi-level-marketing) depends to a great deal on "fake it to make it." To succeed in any MLM, you nearly have to join a cult. (There are some few network marketing organizations which are decent and don't depend on this.)

Up to this point, it's meant a personal belief system which you "infect" others to believe in as much as you. And then get them to infect others the same way. Starting with friends and family.

Nothing has the failure rate that MLM has as a single industry. Because the few who can really motivate masses to follow their lead are just one in a million.

Network Marketing is built on the backs of people who want to start a home business, but don't have a clue. (Not that it can't be done, but this industry is led by the blind.)

The Internet has both been the blessing and downfall of these schemes. Because MLM can now reach people easier than ever, they now have a faster turnover and higher failure rate than ever before.

It's taken this deep study of copywriting to separate out these facts from the fluff.

There are a *huge* number of people out there who are wannabe's. They make their living putting on a show, because they know the bulk of the people out there won't spend the time they need to invest to really learn and apply this or any subject. Such marketers are the ones who popularize the "get rich quick concept," *even though they know it's false.* They also tell you marketing is just a numbers racket – and build spam empires from short-cuts.

Those who win in copywriting study the leaders who have done the testing and found what really works, every time.

Those who are the effective trainers have built courses based on people who have done the testing to prove what works – hundreds, if not thousands of cases.

Follow the really real, the ones that make sense.

Follow the ones who have tested and know.

How to Use this Book to Get Everything You Could Possibly Want

THERE IS A SIMPLE REASON this postscript is at the back of every book in this series:

You need to study all these books to become the best marketer you can.

Because, even mediocre and mis-trained copywriters writing for cheesy products can become millionaires with a few hackneyed, trite "formulas."

The reason I undertook this study was that one example I used earlier – the marketer who was more fake than real. All he really did was to succumb to the easy money being made in Internet Marketing, when you have these "guru's" who have amassed huge lists selling essentially junk to people who would buy it on hope. Then they would cross-sell each other's products to their lists and the cycle would continue with any new product any of them came out with.

Problem was – they weren't actually helping anyone really improve their life.

Here's the proven breakdown of what happens with a training product "guaranteed to make you a millionaire from your own home business" -

• Only 3% of the people who buy the product will actually finish the course.

• 3% of *those* will actually apply what they learned to break even.

• 3% of *those* will become an outrageous success – usually due to having already been trained by several previous training courses they took, not just this one.

The result – 1 in 1,000 will make their money back. 1 in 10,000 will become an flaming success and wind up as an example on infomercials. (With 9,999 chances for refunds.)

But you are different.

In just this short postscript, I've told you everything you need to know in order to make very successful copywriting. The motivations and explanations for why humankind think and act as they do isn't found in any other book. (Well, just the one I wrote on "Get Your Self Scam Free.")

Because I wrote that book after I'd gotten scammed and wanted to find out why so it never happened again.

Scammers use the same techniques as honest marketers. It's just how they go about it.

An old adage about advertising says that great advertising with a poor product will run that company out of business. Mediocre advertising with a great product will make incredible amounts of money.

You can have everything you ever wanted if you

• Have a great product,

• Market it honestly,

• Write your copy brilliantly.

The copywriter's job is to get that product repaired if it's flawed.

Otherwise, you are going to have to find another client – that company isn't going to be around for very long once people find out that the product sucks.

Know what you want out of your own journey-story before you start down that path with any old company willing to hire you.

Get an honest company with a great product and then promote it to the heavens – then watch whatever you really want in life show up.

Too simple. It's the reason that "Honesty is the Best Policy" is still retold today.

You have a right to everything you earn.

Do good – and earn everything you could want.

Did You Find the Strange Secret in This Book?

ALL OUR BOOKS REFERENCE a strange secret. In their own words.

With complete certainty, I can tell you now – from my more than half-century of existence:

- Any and all of my successes, as well as all my disappointments are directly traced to the principles in this book I want to give you.

- For any set-back or failure, I either didn't know these principles, didn't understand their power, or simply ignored them.

- For every success, I have tracked back to taking these exact steps laid out in this book - to achieve, acquire, or attain whatever it was I wanted to be or have.

And that experience is why I produced this short book you can have - to carry with you and review regularly.

You may have heard about it:

"The Strangest Secret Collection" inspired by the works of Earl Nightingale.

This collection contains "The Strangest Secret" transcript by Earl Nightingale, plus selections from other related books.

Limited Time Offer

You can download your own copy of this book –

as long as its still available.

Visit: https://gum.co/SSC-Giveaway

Related Books You May Like

ALL OUR LATEST RELEASES[1]

Both fiction and non-fiction – each with links to major online book outlets as well as author discounts.

Modern Parables[2]

Our short stories and anthologies – all in order of most recent release.

Classic Fiction[3]

Our ever-expanding collection of fiction stories that are hard to find, yet their stories never grow old. Perfect entertainment when the too-modern world becomes stale...

The Strangest Secret Library[4]

All the full references mentioned in Earl Nightingale's Strangest Secret Library available for instant download – through your online book outlet of choice or with our publisher's discount.

Publishing[5]

Our collection of modern and classic references on how to improve your writing in our modern self-publishing age.

Books on Success and Goal Achievement[6]

---

1. https://livingsensical.gumroad.com/?sort=newest

2. https://livingsensical.gumroad.com/?sort=newest&tags=fiction

3. https://livingsensical.gumroad.com/?query=golden%20age&sort=page_layout

4. https://livingsensical.gumroad.com/?query=strangest%20secret&sort=page_layout

5. https://livingsensical.gumroad.com/?query=publishing&sort=page_layout

Our collection of modern and classic references on how you can become a personal success and achieve your own goals – to get everything you want out of life.

Visit https://store.livingsensical.com/ to find the book you're looking for

Libraries of Interest

OUR NO-COST LIBRARIES

Over the years, we've aggregated several top-selling books that people find useful. And mainly, the books we have fit into a handful of categories. For your use, we've built these into libraries, which are all no-charge sign-ups to access PDF versions of these top-selling books:

1. Completely Change Your Life Library:

https://livingsensical.gumroad.com/l/ChangeYourLifeLibrary

(Goal Achievement)

You can have and be anything you want. You can get everything you want out of life. In this library are the tips and tricks to make it all happen for you.

2. Becoming a Writer Library:

https://livingsensical.gumroad.com/l/BecomingAWriterLibrary [1]

(Writing Craft)

There are time-tested and proven methods of writing that leave you refreshed at the end of your writing day – or whatever time you have for it. Writing can be simple, a joy, and bring you peace...

3. Breakthrough Advertising Library:

https://livingsensical.gumroad.com/l/BecomingAWriterLibrary
(Copywriting)

---

1. https://livingsensical.gumroad.com/l/BecomingAWriterLibrary

When you know how people want to be talked to, your ads can help them find the products or services they want. Helping people live better lives isn't full of gimmicky sales tricks. Just stuff that works.

4. Regenerative Agriculture Library:

https://livingsensical.gumroad.com/l/RationalGrazingLibrary (Regenerative Agriculture)

Farming can improve the soil while it supports the families that tend it. It can raise more produce if you plant, graze, and harvest with Nature's proven principles.

5. The Insiders Club:

https://livingsensical.gumroad.com/l/InsidersClub

(Fiction Readers)

For loyal fans – get inside scoops on how these books were written, advance copies for review, and become First Readers – who hear about the stories as they are created. Plus, full Book Universe Notes to get more out of each of our books. For insiders only.

ALL THESE LIBRARIES are live and no-cost to join. Each has around a half-dozen or more of our top-selling books (as PDF's) are in each of these areas for you. Sign up for the ones you want. Simple entertainment or how to fix things in problem areas.

Sign Up Now.

Don't Miss Out!

Want to keep up to date with this author and all upcoming books?

Find out about special discounts?

Hear about pre-release specials, new audiobooks and courses?!?

Instant Access – Join Here

Visit: **https://livingsensical.gumroad.com/l/InsidersClub**

Did You Like This Book?

HOW ABOUT LEAVING A review with the vendor?

Otherwise (or in addition) you can leave your recommendations on:

- Bookbub[1] (https://www.bookbub.com/recommendations)

The whole point is to enable others to find books that you liked reading.

Which then helps you find more great books to read.

And...

Feel free to share this book!

---

1. https://www.bookbub.com/recommendations

Did you love *The Robert Collier Copywriting Course: Second Edition*?
Then you should read *Breakthrough Copywriter 2.0: An Advertising
Field Guide to Eugene M. Schwartz' Classic*[2] by Dr. Robert C. Worstell!

[3]

**There was one copywriter who made millionaires from people who
read his book, but never wrote an ad.**

You may or may not have heard of Eugene M. Schwartz - one of the
most successful copywriters in advertising history.

He worked three hours a day and you couldn't pay him any amount
to write your copy.

Seriously.

At one point he wrote up just how he did it. And never wrote about
that subject ever again.

---

2. https://books2read.com/u/47r7OR

3. https://books2read.com/u/47r7OR

Eugene Schwartz wrote a classic on copywriting almost 50 years ago that is probably one of the most powerful, and profitable, books on copywriting and marketing ever written.

That book has been kept available only as a rare hardback gift edition. Generations of copywriters haven't had access to this material. And the world would be a poorer place, except...

Fortunately, Schwartz was also prolific as a speaker.

*So we are able to bring notes of his lectures and a precise analysis of his classic text to you to make your **own** millions with.*

In this short review guide, you can learn:

How to create ads which sell your products at the expense of your competitionFind which roles your customer really wants to play - and will pay *anything* to get - and align these to your productDiscover how to get a product to sell no matter how people have already heard about it or how many products like it are already out there.Learn how to control your ad-copy viewers by being their honest, trusted friend.

This tribute to his genius is also a guidebook so you can duplicate his success with your own copywriting.

Please enjoy this journey to greater ease and profit. The genius of Eugene Scwartz can teach you, starting immediately.

Scroll Up and Get Your Copy Now.

Read more at https://store.livingsensical.com/?query=worstell&sort=page_layout.

Also by Dr. Robert C. Worstell

Becoming A Writer
Dorothea Brande's Becoming A Writer Collection
PLOTTO Genie: The Endless Story

Change Your Life
How to Completely Change Your Life in 30 Seconds, Second Edition

Change Your Life Toolset
Get Your Self Scam Free

Make Yourself Great Again Library
Why You Got All That Stuff
The Art of Wonk, Compleat

Masters of Copywriting
Breakthrough Copywriter 2.0: An Advertising Field Guide to Eugene
M. Schwartz' Classic

Claude C. Hopkins' Scientific Advertising With My Life in Advertising
The Robert Collier Copywriting Course: Second Edition

Mindset Stacking Guides
Make Yourself Great Again Part 1
Make Yourself Great Again Part 2
Make Yourself Great Again Part 3
Make Yourself Great Again Part 4
Choose. Believe. Win.
Make Yourself Great Again - Complete Collection
Go Thunk Yourself, Again!
The Strangest Secret Collection 2.0
Think Less and Grow Richer
Freedom Is (Period.) 2.0
Seek and Find

PMA Science of Success
Napoleon Hill's PMA: Science of Success Course - An Introduction

Really Simple Writing & Publishing
How To Write And Publish For Free
Backwards Book Publishing: Save Time, Earn More, Work Less
Writing-Publishing Survival Guide
Author Freedom Guidebook
How to Stop Feeding the Beast
How I Survived My First Year of Fiction Writing
Learning from the Pulp Masters: 2nd Edition

How to Become an Instant Author in 30 Seconds
Carolyn Wells' Mystery Story Technique for Writers, Second Edition
Becoming a Wealthy Writer
Marketers & Writers - Scammers & Dupes
How to Write Less and Profit More - Version 2.0
Writing Serial Fiction In the Real World 2.0

Regenerative Agriculture
Grass Productivity: Rational Grazing, Second Edition

Thrive Learning Life Improvement
Avoiding Online Dating Pitfalls

Standalone
Farm Less, Profit More: Lessons in Regenerative Grazing

Watch for more at
https://store.livingsensical.com/?query=worstell&sort=page_layout.

Also by Robert Collier

Masters of Copywriting
The Robert Collier Copywriting Course: Second Edition

About the Publisher

Midwest Journal Press
Finding You Books that Continue to Change Your Life

"**Finding you books that continue to change your life.**"

A veteran publishing imprint and a practical philosophy for life, Midwest Journal Press has been active publishing new and established authors since 2006.

We take advantage of the new Print on Demand and ebook technologies to enable wider discovery for authors.

We publish in most of the major genres of fiction and non-fiction.

Our current emphasis is in speculative fiction modern parables.

Find out about our new releases, publisher discounts, and special offers...

Sign Up Now:
http://store.livingsensical.com/follow

www.ingramcontent.com/pod-product-compliance
Lightning Source LLC
Chambersburg PA
CBHW031300160726
47993CB00001B/244